WHITETAIL SUMMER

WHITETAIL SUMMER

SEASONS OF THE WHITETAIL
BOOK FOUR

Text by John J. Ozoga

WILLOW CREEK PRESS
Minocqua, Wisconsin

PHOTOGRAPHY:
Mark Raycroft, pp. 2, 18, 78, 144.
Jeff Richter, pp. 5, 86, 93, 96, 112.
Leonard Lee Rue, III, p. 8, 80.
Bill Lea, pp. 10, 20, 27, 28, 29, 30, 35, 36, 50-51, 56, 63, 64, 76, 79, 97, 98, 120.
Lance Krueger, pp. 11, 39, 43, 70, 82, 83, 88, 104.
Charles J. Alsheimer, pp. 12, 21, 22, 40, 49, 53, 54, 67, 68, 69, 73, 74, 101, 113, 127, 130, 131.
Donald M. Jones, pp. 14, 17, 32, 42, 60, 77, 87r, 119, 138.
Len Rue, Jr., p. 24.

Denver Bryan, pp. 25, 58, 94.
Mike Blair, pp. 37, 108.
Richard P. Smith, p. 44, 90, 102, 116, 123.
Jeanne Drake, pp. 46, 47, 114.
Henry F. Zeman, p. 61.
Bill Marchel, pp. 62, 91, 107, 111, 117.
Gary L. Alt, pp. 84, 87l, 124, 125, 128, 136, 137, 140, 141.
Steve Lewis, pp. 105, 122, 129, 133.
Greg Gersbach, p. 118.

ISBN 1-57223-044-4

Published by WILLOW CREEK PRESS
P.O. Box 147, Minocqua, WI 54548

Designed by Patricia Bickner Linder

For information on other Willow Creek titles, write or call 1-800-850-WILD.

Printed in Canada

Library of Congress Cataloging-in-Publication Data

Ozoga, John J.
    Whitetail summer / by John J. Ozoga : foreword by Leonard Lee Rue III.
        p.   cm. -- (Seasons of the whitetail : book 4)
    Includes bibliographical references.
    1. White-tailed deer. 2. Summer.   I. Title.   II. Series: Ozoga, John J. Seasons of the whitetail : bk. 4.
QL737.U55O966   1997
599.65'2--dc21   97-1060
                                                            CIP

ACKNOWLEDGEMENTS

Writing the *Seasons of the Whitetail* series of books has been more than an interesting endeavor; it's been a once-in-a-lifetime opportunity that came about strictly by accident. If not for one timely phone call to editor Chuck Petrie, I doubt very much if I would have had the privilege of writing *Whitetail Autumn*, *Whitetail Winter*, *Whitetail Spring*, and now *Whitetail Summer*. Thanks, Chuck, for initiating this effort and for editing all four books.

No man has done more to educate the American public to the ways of white-tailed deer than Leonard Lee Rue III. Through his seminars, books, hundreds of magazine articles, thousands of photographs and, more recently, videos, he has conveyed deer biology in a straight-forward, easily understood fashion to millions of people. Through his educational efforts, I suspect Lennie has benefited sound deer management more than any individual in the business. He honored me and other deer researchers with a very special tribute in the preface to his very popular and recently updated book *The Deer of North America*. And, now, I am deeply honored to have him provide the foreword to *Whitetail Summer*. Lennie, I wish I had just a fraction of your energy, enthusiasm, and communicative skills.

It's one thing to have a book published, of course, but quite another to inform the intended audience of its availability. In my case, I was blessed with the cooperation of some fine members of the news media. I'm deeply indebted to Buck LeVasseur, Bob Garner, James Ford, Mike Avery, and David John for some excellent TV and radio coverage of the first three books in this series. I've also been fortunate to receive some very complimentary written reviews from Jim Casada, Bob Dalpra, Wilson Eedy, Fred Egloff, Ed Erickson, Bob Gwizdz, Nick Karas, Lydia Lohrer, Dave Otto, Dave Richey, Dave Schneider, Dan Schmidt, Eric Sharp, Richard Smith, and, no doubt, others that I am unaware of. Thanks to all of you for your kind words.

I'd also like to thank my family. Most of all, Jan, thanks for helping with the numerous tasks that accompany a project such as this, and for the sacrifices you made while I struggled in putting this story to words. To my mother and father, daughter Holly, sons John, Mark, and Keith, thanks for helping to promote these books and for just being yourselves.

Books like these aren't the type one writes based entirely upon personal experience. I haven't actually counted them, but I've probably cited the works of more than 200 authors in the "Selected References" of this series. I am grateful to those listed, and to many others like them, for contributing to our understanding of whitetails and for providing the knowledge that has made these books possible.

A special thank you to publisher Tom Petrie and the rest of the Willow Creek Press staff, as well as to the photographers whose works adorn these pages. You've helped put together a product all of us can be proud of.

DEDICATION

In memory of the Cusino enclosure deer herd
(1952-1994), for permitting me to watch, to measure,
to ponder, and to learn.

*"We have long stood as foes, hunter and hunted, but now
that is changed and we stand face to face, fellow creatures
looking into each other's eyes, not knowing each other's
speech — but knowing motives and feelings. Now I
understand you as I never did before; surely you at least in
part understand me."*

—Ernest Thompson Seton (1899).

FOREWORD

by Leonard Lee Rue III

I never met a person from whom I couldn't learn something.

I have been in "hot pursuit" of the white-tailed deer since I saw my first deer tracks back on the family farm in 1939. Since that time, I have taken over 200,000 photographs of whitetails, recorded over 200 hours of video, written hundreds of columns and articles, written three books, and given hundreds of lectures and seminars on the white-tailed deer. Yet, every time I go out to video deer, I learn something new. Each new observation may be just an insignificant little tidbit, or of interest to no one but myself, but it adds to my fund of knowledge and may actually be the one piece needed to complete the puzzle. When I discover something that really puzzles me, a piece that I need help on, I call on my friends who are top research biologists. I frequently call on John Ozoga.

I have never met John personally, but we often communicate via letter or phone. I have admired John's research work for years and am pleased that he is now making it available to the general

In summer, whitetail bucks' antlers grow at an almost implausible pace. The tender, growing appendages will become hardened implements of battle by autumn.

public and that he is doing it with a flair. His books are educational, informative, and enjoyable to read.

I was pleased when John asked me to write the foreword to this book because I consider it an honor to be a part of this series. John's *Seasons of the Whitetail* series is a must for anyone wanting to know more about America's favorite game animal. There is something here for everyone: the nature enthusiast, the deer hunter, the game managers and, yes, other biologists, too.

"Tis summer and the livin' is easy."

Summer is the one time of the year when a whitetail can actually take it easy for a short while. Spring is the time of birth and antler regrowth. It's a time of playing catch-up after the rigors of winter have passed. Autumn is the hectic season when there is an urgency about everything. Mandatory lipogenesis demands that all deer cram in carbohydrates to layer fat upon their bodies in preparation for winter. The rut and the breeding season has the entire deer world in a turmoil. Winter is all about survival.

Even in the summer, a whitetail has to be constantly on the alert for danger; there is no respite from that. "Eternal vigilance is the price of life." However, the deer's population peaks in June; it is at the apex, its zenith, and although the increase is made up of fawns, the sheer number of fawns reduces the amount of predation on the entire herd.

In summer, does are busy with their fawns, and nursing places a tremendous drain upon deer mothers, but the vegetation is growing profusely and, in early summer, it is higher in protein than at any other time of the year. Although the fawns are dependent upon their mother's milk for at least six weeks, they start to eat vegetation from the day they are born. A fawn's increase in size does not put a greater drain on the doe, however, as the fawn's intake of vegetation increases proportionately with its growth.

For doe whitetails, summer is a period of abundant food, but it is also a season devoted to the responsibilities of raising fawns and a new generation of deer.

The buck's antlers finish their growth in late July and solidify throughout the month of August, with the peeling of the velvet taking place in the first part of September. During the antler-growing period, bucks move no more, and travel no farther, then they absolutely have to. The intensity of summer heat has much to do with restricting the buck's daily range, but the main reason bucks confine their movements is to avoid damaging their growing antlers.

The deer's summer coat is a model of efficiency with its short, solid hairs. Despite this, the deer do not move about in sun-drenched meadows, farmlands, and open areas. When they do move about in the daylight hours, they will do so only in wooded areas. Because they avoid the heat of the day, the deer are active for much longer periods at night.

John explains all of these factors in great detail, spelling them out so that they can easily be understood by the lay reader and biologist alike. Indeed, reading *Whitetail Summer* will benefit all of us, as well as the deer.

Leonard Lee Rue III
Blairstown, NJ

PREFACE

Without any stretch of the imagination, white-tailed deer are this country's ultimate wildlife success story — in some cases they've been too successful. While many species floundered in the wake of human progress, whitetails, owing largely to their extreme adaptiveness and opportunistic nature, have flourished — indeed, they are different.

Despite their current high numbers and widespread distribution, however, the whitetails' future is not absolutely secure. Many whitetail populations are not healthy, for one reason or another, and some of us are more than a bit concerned with the way deer populations are managed and what the future may hold for them.

Escalating deer numbers, fewer natural predators, human encroachment into natural environments, along with ill conceived deer harvest and forest management strategies — often based on emotional human demands and economics instead of sound biological reasoning — have contributed to

Although not as gregarious as other deer species, whitetails of both sexes and all ages gather in complex social groups at certain times of the year.

The widely distributed whitetail invites human attention more than any member of North America's deer family.

many deer populations that are now socially as well as nutritionally out of balance. In fact, in some sections of the country, due to an overabundance of female deer, induced by human interests, whitetails have attained "pest" status. That's a sad commentary for such a noble animal.

Meanwhile there is a strong "naturalism" movement on the horizon. In the future, management of forests and wildlife on public lands will likely place greater emphasis on biodiversity, on maintaining old-growth forest stands, on utilizing ecological approaches to resource management, and producing plant and animal communities more like those that existed prior to the white man's arrival on this continent. How these changes will impact white-tailed deer, which do best in early vegetational stages, is unknown.

It was not my purpose in this series of books to dwell upon the virtues of sport hunting for deer, to debate the desirability of one deer harvest or forest management strategy over another, or to ponder the whitetails' probable future. But these are important issues that should concern all of us who really care about the long-term welfare of white-tailed deer — issues that cannot be ignored.

Today, deer hunting, or lack there of, represents one of the most potent forces regulating deer abundance and shaping herd sex-age composition. Great strides have been made in deer management in recent years, but even now, in many parts of the country, deer management remains primarily a political football because a poorly informed public permits it.

In the past, poorly informed deer hunters were the most vocal group blocking progressive, scientifically sound deer management practices. In the future, however, the non-hunting public — the vast majority of our population, some of which will be swayed by anti-hunting sentiment — will more likely play a prominent role in dictating deer management policies, thereby determining the welfare of whitetails over extensive areas. In the future, votes by a poorly informed and uneducated public could be a serious threat to biologically sound deer management.

In the absence of effective natural predators, I believe that regulated deer hunting is necessary for the good of the species, especially when one considers the alternative natural population control measures (i.e., disease, malnutrition, long-term damage to the habitat, etc.). However, it is my contention that hunting should be employed more effectively as a management tool with the whitetails' long-term welfare utmost in mind, not as an end in itself — recreational interests should not dictate deer management policy. Although some wildlife

managers will disagree with me, it is my immediate concern that we strive more seriously to manage whitetail populations in the same manner in which they evolved — nutritionally and socially balanced.

The near complete harvesting of antlered bucks as occurs annually in some sections of the country, in conjunction with minimal harvesting of female deer, produces unbalanced deer populations that, in my view, are far from being natural or healthy. I believe hunters should become more selective harvesters and inflict mortality that more closely mimics natural predation, not only to hold deer populations in numerical balance with existing food and cover, but also to produce populations that are in social harmony. Macho ego aside, sometimes it may be more beneficial to bypass the buck and harvest a doe, or maybe even a fawn.

Clearly, hunters' attitudes must change from an emphasis on personal goals to valuing their role in deer management, with a sincere concern for the whitetails' long-term healthful existence utmost in mind. Equally important, however, is that the general public become more knowledgeable regarding the whitetails' social and nutritional needs, learn how those demands relate to the animals' well being, and more willingly support biologically sound management practices that perpetuate healthy deer populations. We, the hunting and non-hunting public, have immense political clout when it comes to determining wildlife management direction; all too often, however, we do not wisely exercise that power.

I can only echo the sentiments voiced by Leonard Rue III in his book *The Deer of North America*: "The greatest and most difficult task still confronting wildlife managers is that of educating the general public, hunters included." As Leonard rightfully criticized, "The general public is not being reached; the reports and recommendations of the game biologists are not being read and understood."

A little over 10 years ago, my wife, Janice, addressed this issue most succinctly when she told me, "You research biologists spend all your time talking to yourselves." Unfortunately, she was right. Although there are some notable exceptions (Valerius Geist, David Guynn, Harry Jacobson, Larry Marchinton, Dave Mech, and Karl Miller, to name a few), most wildlife researchers do not bother to translate their technical reports into popular print for the general public.

Many wildlife managers, on the other hand, often view research findings as parochial or provincial, in that the results only apply to the region and circumstances under which the studies were conducted. "That's not how things work in my area" is not an uncommon response, or excuse, to ignore new research findings.

Still other managers go overboard in response to public opinion by trying to manage deer populations in a manner that is politically acceptable, but sometimes biologically disastrous. Obviously, their political approach has nothing to do with sound resource management. Wildlife managers should play a strong leadership role in responsible deer management — they are the trained stewards of this valuable resource and don't get paid to tell people what they want to hear.

This series, *Seasons of the Whitetail,* has provided me with a rare opportunity and a sizable challenge to put together a wealth of factual information for the benefit of those who share my deep concern for this remarkable creature, the white-tailed deer. I admit that I am biased in certain of my views, and certainly don't pretend to know everything there is to know about whitetails—no one does. Be that as it may, within these pages lies my current thinking. I hope those who study these books, and ponder my message, will come away somewhat wiser and more willing to support management policies that have the white-tailed deer's best interests utmost in mind.

— John J. Ozoga

The highly adaptable whitetail can eke out a living in a variety of environments, from suburban areas, where they live in close proximity to humans, to vast stretches of wilderness.

CONTENTS

INTRODUCTION

I f there is any truly tranquil time in the life of a prey species such as the white-tailed deer, it occurs in the warm months of summer. During June, July, and August, over most of the whitetail's geographical range, the weather is pleasant and the landscape is dominated by lush green vegetation. Dense plant growth provides deer with plentiful cover that hides them from predators (especially important for vulnerable young fawns), protection from the elements during brief periods of inclement weather, and, most importantly, an abundant supply of nutritious forage.

For most whitetails, summer is a season of plenty — a season of fruition, of growth and development. It is a season of frolicking spotted fawns, sleek red-coated does, and mild mannered bucks with bulging velvet antlers. It is a time when deer are preoccupied with finding large quantities of nutritious forage — when eating governs their daily routine and is of utmost priority.

In summer, whitetail bucks build body mass and protect their tender, growing antlers. Reserve energy supplies and antler size will partly determine their breeding success during the autumn rut.

Whitetail fawn births are timed to occur during periods of lush vegetative growth. This not only provides nourishing foods for young deer and their mothers, it also supplies fawns with abundant hiding cover.

In summer, a doe nursing fawns must consume copious amounts of food high in energy, protein, and essential minerals and vitamins, so that she can produce plenty of milk, necessary if her fawns are to achieve rapid growth and maximum size prior to winter. Meanwhile, adult bucks are growing new antlers, replacing spent body tissues, and building fat stores of reserve energy in preparation for the energetically expensive breeding season.

The whitetail's social habits and activity patterns are dynamic and change markedly with the seasons. Although whitetails may frequent open areas, they are not plains animals; they spend most of their time in dense forest cover. They are also considered to be the least gregarious member of the deer family, Cervidae. Nonetheless, they exhibit highly complex social habits, which are largely governed by their stage of reproduction and change rather dramatically with the seasons. The adult sexes form separate, highly structured societies and live apart during most of the summer season.

Early summer is when whitetails are most widely and evenly distributed across their range. It is a time when the screening effects of green foliage make it seem as if deer were absent in areas where they live at low densities. This will gradually change, however, as summer progresses.

During the coarse of summer, newborn fawns develop rapidly, from vulnerable infants dependent upon their mother's milk for sustenance to self-sufficient ruminants. By late summer, fawns no longer spend most of their time in hiding. They become more active and develop daily activity patterns and social habits more like those of their mothers and older relatives.

As their fawns become stronger and more capable of fleeing from predators, nursing does become more amiable and abandon their agonistic, territorial behavior associated with raising young fawns. With their young close at heel, adult does begin to associate in groups with female kin and their fawns, groups that normally occupy closely aligned ranges. Soon the young fawns will interact with other deer and learn what the whitetail's social life is all about.

Adult bucks become more active during late summer too. They'll leave their favored early summer haunts to mingle with family groups of does and fawns, and to cavort with unfamiliar bucks. By then the bucks' velvet antlers have started to harden; it won't be long before the antler-growth process will be completed and the mature antlers shed their velvety outer covering, all in anticipation of the pending breeding season.

Indeed, with few exceptions, summer is a good time for whitetails. But, of course, there are exceptions;

By late summer, bucks' antlers will harden and the velvet covering will be stripped, revealing what will become, in part, each buck's identifying signature.

summer is not completely without peril, and it is not always kind to whitetails in all regions of the country.

Not all habitat types are favorable to deer. Areas of inherently poor soils, for example, produce forage of low nutritive value. Also, drought, floods, wild fires, a lack of nutritious forage (often the result of foraging by too many deer), and human destruction of natural habitats periodically create hardship.

Shortages in the quantity or quality of summer deer foods may produce only subtle deleterious effects and go completely unnoticed to the untrained eye. Or, on the other hand, food shortage during summer may be so severe as to impact the health and well-being of whitetails over vast areas. In either case, lack of proper nutrition during summer may set the stage for widespread injurious consequences and may ultimately govern the health and abundance of whitetails in some areas.

The combination of heat stress and drought as sometimes occurs in the Southwest, in areas like the Llano Basin of Texas, for example, may be just as devastating to whitetails as the intense cold and deep snow that characterize fierce winters in the northern Great Lakes region. Just as harsh winter weather may contribute to food shortage, malnutrition, and death of deer on northern range, so might inadequate rainfall and lack of soil moisture limit the growth of nutritious forage and impact the well-being of whitetails on southern range.

In the Southwest, wet and dry periods may last for several years and govern range carrying capacities for deer (and livestock) accordingly. Lack of soil moisture greatly reduces the abundance and nutrient value of plant growth. The resultant food shortage and malnutrition cause slow body growth among young deer, delay their onset of sexual maturity, result in low conception rates among does the next autumn, and can contribute to high mortality during the winter season. Hot summer weather also opens the door to parasites and disease, especially among malnourished animals living in crowded conditions. And without dense, low-level hiding cover, young fawns become more vulnerable to roving predators.

Natural predators such as the wolf, mountain lion, black bear, bobcat, and coyote always pose a potential threat to whitetails wherever predator and prey co-exist. Given the opportunity, predators are always alert to removing the vulnerable young, sick, weak, and less wary whitetails.

During summer, however, all these selective forces are far less operative than at other times of the year — unless, of course, environmental circumstances, human interference, or deer overabundance contribute to habitat degradation and a shortage of food and cover.

Regardless of the stresses they may face, whitetails in each region of the country have evolved to cope with whatever adversities prevail in those locales. The superior, best adapted whitetails always somehow manage to survive.

Today, whitetails are no longer strictly inhabitants of remote, heavily forested regions; as never before, the white-tailed deer, a symbol of wilderness, has expanded its range and now populates every conceivable niche of favorable habitat. There is no other big game animal on this continent that touches the lives of more people. While doing so, the whitetail now makes a nuisance of itself in some areas of farmlands and in sprawling suburban landscapes where its prolific presence sometimes results in destructive consequences.

Indeed, to the delight of some people but the trepidation of others, white-tailed deer are this nation's ultimate wildlife success story.

Habitat quality will largely determine the hardiness of the whitetails inhabiting it. Marginal habitats, such as this sea coast with its scrub vegetation, are generally less favorable for whitetail subsistence.

SOCIETAL STRUCTURE

P atterns of white-tailed deer (*Odocoileus virginianus*) social behavior evolved in response to predators, disease, habitat, climate, hunting by Native Americans, and probably many other constantly changing pressures. The resultant behavior system is geared to help provide whitetails the basic necessities of life, including exploitation of resources (food, cover, and water), predator avoidance, mating, and the rearing of young. Clearly, the whitetail's social organization is an adaptation that is genetically inherited and critical to the species' healthful existence.

In his famous book *A Herd of Red Deer*, naturalist Fraser Darling made the following assessment: "Where a species is of social habit, I would emphasize the necessity of taking sociality fully into account in observing and interpreting behavior."

Although Darling made the following statement specifically with regard to red deer, it applies equally well to whitetails: "The life-history of the [white-tailed deer] would be an empty

Among bucks, establishing dominance over other males is a biological imperative. In summer, when bucks antlers are sensitive and still in velvet, intimidation displays, rather than fighting, suffice to keep upstart males in their place.

The size and rate of growth of antlers in young bucks is determined in part by the timing of their birth, by the quality of their diet, and by genetic factors.

and meaningless thing divorced from the sociality which is the very foundation of their existence."

While not as gregarious as some ungulates, white-tailed deer are by no means antisocial; they are highly social beings that live in complex social arrangements. As opposed to an animal "aggregation," where individuals interact much at random, members of a whitetail population interact as a "society" and function cooperatively. Socially compatible animals recognize one another and communicate effectively. This helps to minimize tension and stress, provides for an orderly and efficient way of life, increases survivability, and assures genetic fitness within the population.

The whitetail's world is a very competitive one. Things such as dominance rank and the existence of social alliances sometimes determine whether a particular deer lives or dies. Therefore, deer density, herd sex-age composition, genetic relationships, and other factors that determine a deer's social environment can have profound effects upon deer behavioral patterns in any given area.

As with other ungulates, whitetails exhibit sexual segregation. This means that adult bucks and does live separately — spatially and socially — except during the breeding season. Females live in matriarchal groups composed of related individuals, whereas bucks

(generally unrelated) live in all-male, or fraternal, groups. Such separation is most pronounced during the late spring and early summer period, when adult bucks are growing antlers and does are raising fawns. In fact, whitetail bucks differ so dramatically from does in so many aspects of their life history that one must wonder how such differences came to be in the first place.

Female whitetails may spend their entire lifetime on familiar ancestral range in close association with related females. At some point, however, the male must sever ties with his mother and female relatives. When sexually mature, the young buck is harassed, dominated, and rejected by his female kin. He has little choice but to seek out, interact with, and achieve compatible associations with other males. In effect, it has been said of whitetails, that one can "treat the sexes as if they were different species."

Although some behaviorists may disagree with me, I, for lack of a better term, choose to refer to the whitetails' separate matriarchal and fraternal social units as "societies." In doing so, I admittedly define a society quite broadly as a group of individuals belonging to the same species and organized in a cooperative manner. In my view, then, society members recognize one another, communicate and interact quite frequently, and live cooperatively in a highly organized and structured social arrangement.

As they apply to deer population management, sociobiological principles are seldom considered in this country, except in instances where "quality deer management" is practiced. However, European big game managers emphasize the importance of understanding species societal structure and strive to maintain game populations that are in social balance as well as nutritional balance. Such management rests on the premise that populations must be in social harmony — that is, they must have a proper sex-age composition as well as live within the carrying capacity of the range if they are to remain healthy.

Conversely, according to European philosophy, improper deer harvesting can distort the social structure of a population, leading to behavioral disruption and chaos. Social disorder presumably spawns excitement and hyperactivity, contributing to higher than normal food requirements, poor physical condition, low productivity, increased mortality, and, ultimately, severe damage to the habitat.

In ungulates, individuals occur in distinct social classes determined by each animal's degree of physical and behavioral maturity. Classes are hierarchial in nature, with immature animals occupying the lower classes and the most mature occupying the upper classes.

As a result, competition and dominant-submissive relationships have a "suppressor effect" within both the female and male societies. The reproductive performance of lower-ranked animals is restricted due to social domination and intimidation by individuals of higher social standing.

Prime-age animals are considered to be the population's governors of social order. They dominate the younger animals and suppress their aggressive behavior. On the other hand, the overharvest of mature animals tends to upset a given population's so-called "agonistic balance," which leads to social unrest. When mature animals are too few to dampen the aggressiveness of younger members, the resultant strife, excitement, and confusion can become dangerously intense and energetically costly to the society. To restore social order, such an unhealthy condition can only be remedied through selective harvesting of overly abundant individuals (generally from young sex-age classes), and protecting the scarce prime-age individuals.

According to research conducted by the late Anthony Bubenik and other prominent European scientists, most ungulates demonstrate five maturity classes within a society: kids, pre-teens, teens, primes, and seniors. (These are terms taken from human social sciences and which apply to both sexes.) In a smoothly operating and

Unlike their custom in autumn, when bucks lead relatively solitary lives, early summer finds adult male whitetails associating in fraternal groups. At this same time, research has shown does to be more reclusive, especially when their fawns have yet to progress beyond the early hiding stage.

well-structured society, a long-lived individual advances from a young (pre-pubertal) state to peak productivity at prime age, and on to senility at advanced age.

It is important to note, however, that an animal's age alone does not determine its social standing. Nutrition, social relationships, reproductive success, mortality factors, herd sex-age composition and density, and a host of other factors may interact to determine an individual's rate of development and social rank.

While conducting deer research in Michigan's square-mile Cusino enclosure for more than 20 years, I had the rare opportunity to investigate, with precise detail and experimental control enjoyed by few other investigators, the social life of whitetails. Populations within the enclosure were controlled carefully by live-trapping and annually removing surplus animals; individuals returned to the enclosure for study were literally hand picked to meet the needs of specific investigations. Each animal within the enclosure was blood-sampled, measured, weighed, and marked for individual identification. But by far the most valuable data were gathered by X-raying the does in March, to determine fetus numbers and age. Subsequent field observations then allowed us to determine fawn-rearing success, to mark and identify the fawns, and determine mother-young relationships through intensive observations.

Although my interpretation differs somewhat from that reported in European literature, I'm convinced that white-tailed deer can be assigned to one of five social classes based upon their level of physical and behavioral maturity. I also suggest that the sexes represent different societies, differing with regard to those factors determining the social growth and ultimate status of individuals within the respective societies.

THE FEMALE SOCIETY

Female whitetails live within a highly organized matriarchal society wherein related females occupy individual but contiguous fawn-rearing territories. These females socialize with one another and share ancestral range during most of the year.

In order to form and maintain a kinship group that controls a sizeable area of favorable habitat, females within the group must produce daughters that are also successful in rearing offspring. Furthermore, a doe's individual status within the social group hinges heavily upon her reproductive success, and even seemingly subtle details such as breeding date, sex ratio of progeny, and location of fawning sites with respect to those of female relatives will change with social class. These are highly important factors when it comes to maintaining social order and allowing whitetails to exploit food and

Older whitetail mothers, especially those that have successfully raised fawns in the past, are more attentive to and protective of their young than are young, maternally inexperienced does.

cover resources in the most harmonious manner possible.

I suggest that the whitetail female society consists of five social classes, including kids, teens, dispersers, matriarchs (two subclasses), and seniors, as follows:

Class 1 Females: Kids. Female kids are young animals, immature in all respects, still highly dependent upon older females for guidance. They are the most subordinate animals in the population and are likely to suffer severe consequences without adult female guidance. Kids do not breed during their first autumn.

Females remain in the kid class for at least one year, some even longer, depending upon their rate of maturity and achievement of puberty — determined largely by such things as birth date, nutrition, and social pressure. When nutrition is extremely poor or herd density very high, some females could remain in this class for several years.

When one year old, female and male whitetails may band together or temporarily associate with older non-productive female relatives while their mothers raise new fawns. However, they reunite with their mothers as soon as possible.

Logically, this class could be divided into a number of subclasses, based upon the fawns' physical and behavioral development. Regardless, animals in this class are highly susceptible to predation, malnutrition, and other forms of natural mortality.

Class 2 Females: Teens. I consider first-time mothers as being "teens," which probably agrees with the European classification system. Most teens will be two years old when they produce their first litter, but they could be younger or older; however, they would not be fully grown.

Teens are the poorest mothers, more likely to abandon fawns rather than defend them against predators — probably due to their incomplete physiological development as well as maternal inexperience. They tend to give birth several days to several weeks later than older does, and usually establish fawning territories adjacent to their mothers. In some cases, they may benefit from the elder doe's predator defense. Even when well nourished, however, they are likely to lose 20 percent of their newborn. But when severely crowded at high herd density (100 or more deer per square mile), or exposed to intense predation, they may lose more than half of their fawns within a few weeks.

Teens are dominated by older females. If they fail to raise their fawns, they revert to behavior typical of younger females by seeking their mother's companionship as soon as possible. They then behave more like younger females and do not advance beyond this class until they raise at least one fawn.

As a social class, teens would have been the last does to breed during the previous rut. Compared to older, experienced mothers, two-year-old and older females in this class tend to breed a few days to several weeks later, whereas one-year-olds breed about one month later than experienced mothers. However, at least in a northern environment, females less than one year old only breed under the most ideal nutritional conditions and only when the female society is structured heavily in favor of young females, generally due to intensive harvesting of antlerless animals.

(In my enclosure studies, only one of 208 one-year-old females produced a fawn, despite optimal nutrition, likely due to the harsh northern environment and domination by older society members.)

Two- and three-year-olds in this class conceive, on average, 1.4 to 1.7 fetuses. In my studies, those that failed to achieve threshold body weights of 130 pounds prior to breeding (my subjects were the large *borealis* subspecies of white-tailed deer) seldom conceived twins; none carried triplets. Regardless of their age, Class 2 does tend to produce a preponderance (about 60 percent) of male offspring.

Even under the most ideal nutritional circumstances, Class 2 does will produce the smallest male fawns at weaning age, regardless of litter size. Interestingly,

Within doe groups, position within the matriarchal hierarchy determines where each doe will establish her birthing site. Subordinate clan members not adhering to their class position will be challenged by older does when such territorial disputes arise.

The hardiness of a doe's offspring and the chances of her fawns surviving are determined in part by the mother's age and her social position within the female clan.

however, when well-fed, their single female fawns will be as large as those produced by older does.

Class 3 Females: Dispersers. Depending upon habitat availability and herd composition, second-time mothers are likely to shift their fawn-rearing area by dispersing a quarter-mile or so from their birth location. This tends to expand the ancestral range during favorable times when food and cover resources are ideal and related females are increasing in number.

Dispersal is risky, however, because the doe may settle in poor fawning habitat or attempt to usurp the area of a more dominant doe. Depending upon conditions, dispersers may lose 20 percent or more of their newborn, but could lose half of them when predators are abundant. However, if older females are being removed from the population at a high rate, for whatever reason, thereby leaving voids within ancestral range, few second-time mothers would disperse.

When well nourished, does in this class breed earlier than Class 2 does (at about the same time as older, prime-age does), they conceive, on average, about 1.8 fawns per doe and are unique because they usually produce a preponderance of (nearly 60 percent) female fawns. Given the circumstances prompting dispersal, production of excess female offspring by does settling in new habitat is probably adaptive; it allows for more rapid growth of an expanding kinship group when conditions favor population growth.

Although female progeny produced by does in this class tend to be as large as those reared by older females, their male offspring (even singletons) are generally smaller at weaning age. Reasons for such disparity in size are highly speculative. The difference could be due to the benefits some fawns incur from being closely associated with female relatives other than the mother — something scientists refer to as "social facilitation." That is, male fawns raised by dispersing mothers may not have as many female relatives to associate with, and may be more behaviorally restricted in their movements and feeding.

Class 4 Females: Matriarchs. Matriarchs are prime-age, maternally experienced females that generally range from four to about 12 years of age. They are mature in all aspects of physical, physiological, and psychological development. They represent the epitome of health and physical fitness. Matriarchs are the survivors: the hardiest and finest female stock of their species. Matriarchs are also the reproductive machines that permit a population to grow at a maximum rate.

Matriarchs further serve as the social governors of the female society. They are clan leaders by virtue of their long life and ability to produce daughters that also survive. Based upon my observations of this social class during my enclosure research, I chose to divide these females into two distinct subclasses—secondary matriarchs and primary matriarchs—according to differences in the complexity of their matriarchies.

Secondary matriarchs are females that successfully dispersed only within the last year or two; in all likeli-

Prime age does in good health are the engines that drive whitetail populations to maximum size. These matriarchs are not only the most successful mothers in the clan, they are also the social governors of the female society.

hood they are grandmothers. In a rapidly growing deer population they could be quite young, possibly only four or five years old, and serve as leaders for a fairly small subgroup represented by only two or three daughters and their offspring.

Secondary matriarchs usually breed early in the rut and tend to conceive twins, equally split between males and females. They are extremely successful mothers, rarely losing more than 10 percent of their newborn fawns, even when threatened by predators. At weaning age their fawns are superior to those produced by younger does and almost on a par with those reared by older, well-established matriarchs.

In whitetails, primary matriarchs are the true clan leaders; they are great-grandmothers or older; most will be older than six years. Given excellent nutrition and a stable social environment, some may hold their superior social position until the ripe old age of 12 years, or possibly longer. Primary matriarchs tend to be extremely aggressive; they may dominate one or more secondary matriarch daughters, and they travel freely over a large ancestral range.

Healthy primary matriarchs are generally the first does to breed. They usually conceive twins or triplets, with a slight excess (about 55 percent) of male progeny. Because they control the best fawn-rearing habitat and are extremely vigilant and protective mothers, they rarely lose more than 10 percent of their newborn. At weaning age, the male offspring of primary matriarchs tend to be the largest young-of-the-year in the population and may attain enormous size for their age if their littermate(s) succumb early in life.

Matriarch does often give birth to twins or triplets. Also, because they are experienced, protective mothers, matriarchs lose fewer fawns to predators than do younger whitetail mothers.

Class 5 Females: Seniors. The majority of senior females will be 12 years or older, depending upon the severity of climate, nutritional conditions, and probably the individual's reproductive history. Seniors are no longer physically fit, may exhibit hormone imbalances, may lose their high dominance rank, start to breed later than prime-age does, and more likely conceive single males. Because their milk production tends to decline and their fawns are born later, their offspring (especially twins) may be inferior to those raised by prime-age does. Also, because of their late fawning date and loss of dominance, some senior females may be forced to seek new fawning grounds. Beyond 16 years of age, some does fail to breed, especially those living on poor range.

In some populations where female deer are lightly hunted, a surprisingly high number of female whitetails achieve senior status. In central Upper Michigan, for example, researcher Timothy Van Deelen found over 20 percent of the adult females in the wintering herd were older than 12 years. During severe northern winters, senior females may represent a high proportion of the malnutrition-related overwinter deaths. However, given favorable circumstances, even in the wild, some female whitetails live to be 20 years old.

THE MALE SOCIETY

Puberty among whitetail bucks is essentially an annually recurring event, one that has a direct bearing upon their sociability. That is, the male whitetail is a fairly docile, almost frail-appearing, and highly sociable critter during most of the year. Each autumn, however, he becomes a hormonally charged weapon, wielding an awesome mass of muscle — a totally unpredictable beast of amazing strength, stamina, and determination.

Bucks compete aggressively for breeding privileges. Because physical size and strength are important factors determining a buck's dominance status, longevity and good nutrition during the summer season are important factors determining an individual buck's breeding success.

Anyone who has spent time observing whitetails readily recognizes the differences in physical appearance and behavior among bucks of different age groups. Young, sexually inexperienced bucks, for example, are not only smaller in body and antler size when compared with mature individuals, they are also amateurish in their breeding behavior and scurry about and chase females in a disoriented, if not comical, fashion.

By comparison, the finesse and ritualized behavior of a mature rut-experienced buck sporting massive antlers and a rut-swollen neck is a sight to behold. Granted, much of the buck's behavior is instinctive, but his courtship style — including his signposting behavior — steadily improve with experience, learning, and overall maturation.

The only technical paper I've seen referring to specific social maturity classes in white-tailed deer was written by Bennett Brown, Jr., and is based upon studies he conducted on the Rob and Bessie Welder Refuge in Texas. Using radiotelemetry and direct observation, Brown identified four primary association patterns demonstrated by male whitetails: immature, subdominant floaters, group core members, and dominant floaters.

With some modification of Brown's classification system, I suggest that the whitetail's male society consists of the following five classes: kids, subdominant floaters, fraternal group members (two subclasses), dominant floaters, and seniors.

Class 1 Males: Kids. I use the term "kids" here because it is more accurately descriptive than Brown's term "immature." That is, bucks in subsequent classes may be sexually active but not necessarily fully grown or behaviorally mature. Male whitetails usually remain in the kid class, along with female siblings, for at least 12 months.

Even at very young age, male whitetails are inherently more independent, more active, and more inquisitive

Male whitetails are generally not aggressive toward each other in early and mid-summer. Still, minor altercations do take place, some of which involve physical contact.

than females. As a result, after weaning, Class 1 males may socialize frequently with female relatives other than their mother, or possibly even with young bucks.

Most buck fawns (kids) presumably do not achieve puberty. However, if polished "infant" antlers signify puberty, and they probably do, then some whitetail populations produce more sexually active buck fawns than others. In my enclosure studies, for example, when fed nutritious supplemental rations, 84 percent of the buck fawns grew polished antlers less than one-half inch long. For a brief period toward the conclusion of the rut, these precocious males may exhibit "rutty" behavior: They may rub shrubs and trees with their forehead, scent-mark overhead limbs, take special interest in the scrapes and rubs made by older bucks, and sometimes even spar with one another.

Although some six- to eight-month-old buck fawns are capable of breeding in captivity, or possibly even in

highly disturbed populations where older bucks are scarce or absent, it's unlikely that many of them breed in natural populations, due to domination by older males as well as female relatives. Following their initial, relatively short burst of puberty, most buck fawns seek adult female companionship and remain part of the traditional family group throughout winter.

When one year old, Class 1 whitetails, both males and females, are driven away by their mothers when their new fawns are born. The year-old deer then band together and, during summer, travel the corridors between doe fawn-rearing territories on familiar ancestral range. If a mother loses her fawns, she will permit her one-year-old offspring to rejoin her within a few days.

Class 2 Males: Subdominant Floaters. Subdominant floaters are young bucks that have recently left their family social unit, are in some stage of dispersal, but have not yet earned male group

After they are weaned and until they reach puberty, young male whitetails, inherently more inquisitive and active than doe fawns, frequently socialize with female relatives of their mother's clan.

When their mothers give birth to the season's new crop of fawns, one-year-old does and bucks often gather together and travel in groups over their mothers' ancestral range.

membership; most Class 2 males are between one and two years old.

Usually, only about 20 percent of the males disperse from their birth range when one year old. Some leave during summer, but most leave when about 16 months old, shortly before breeding starts in autumn. Probably less than 10 percent of Class 2 males are two and a half years old, meaning they had remained with the family group for one extra year; only rarely would males less than one year old disperse during autumn.

Class 2 males tend to shed antler velvet somewhat later than older bucks, but shortly thereafter seem compelled to search out and interact with other males, generally during late September in the Upper Midwest. Initially, Class 2 bucks spar with other bucks in a rather congenial and highly ritualized fashion, which is probably essential in the formation and maintenance of social bonds among males. Prior to the rut, however, the subdominant floater is likely to travel over an extensive range and interact with various males as well as female groups.

Subdominant floaters are immature in all aspects of physical, physiological, and psychological development. Although they may already have accomplished much of their skeletal growth, even the largest tend to be a third lighter in body weight and carry smaller antlers than older bucks. Physiologically, Class 2 bucks are capable of breeding, but they enter breeding condition later than older males, lag behind older bucks in sex organ development, and attain lower threshold levels of testosterone.

These young bucks tend to be very inquisitive and readily investigate signposts created by older bucks, but do minimal scent-marking themselves. Depending upon their social environment, they make less than half as many antler rubs as do older bucks, and probably make no scrapes when older bucks are present.

In a highly structured male society, Class 2 bucks are dominated by older males. This suppressor effect reduces the young buck's aggressiveness and libido, thereby helping to maintain social order during the breeding season. The behaviorally suppressed young buck also expends less energy, experiences less weight loss during the rut, and therefore grows to greater size at maturity before assuming a herd sire role.

I know of no detailed study regarding fraternal group formation, but my observations indicate most subdominant floaters achieve social bonds with other males during sparring matches prior to the rut, and later spend the winter with them. Some do not find male companions, however, but instead reunite with female relatives and spend the winter with them, becoming

Within fraternal groups, secondary bucks are those males ranging from two and a half to three and a half years old. These deer, although they usually exhibit branched antlers, are not yet fully grown and remain submissive to older bucks within the group.

Whitetail males begin seeking association with older bucks when they reach puberty and are expelled from their mothers' female social groups.

subdominant floaters the next year, when two and a half years old.

Class 3 Males: Fraternal Group Members. Brown suggests the real stability of the male society rests within fraternal groups formed by two to four core members that achieve true social bonds. Generally, these core members are fairly young bucks — probably two and a half to four and a half years old — that have not achieved their maximum body and antler size. However, depending upon herd density and composition, fraternal group members may be as young as one and a half years or as old as five and a half years.

Most true fraternal groups probably have fewer than six members, but members from neighboring groups may share a common range while growing antlers. During late summer and early autumn, in particular, bucks from neighboring groups, as well as subdominant floaters, periodically intermingle to form much larger, but only temporary, male groups.

Although group members frequently spar among themselves and with subdominant floaters, serious aggression among socially bonded members is generally infrequent and not very intense. During the pre-rut period, shortly after antler velvet shedding, these middle-class bucks seem to absorb much of the sparring with subordinate floaters and members of neighboring

fraternal groups, thus somewhat buffering the older "alpha" bucks from excessive, unnecessary energy drainage. Although fraternal group members separate and become solitary travelers during the rut, they quickly regroup after the breeding season and spend the winter together, probably in areas peripheral to concentrations of does and fawns.

Because bucks within established fraternal groups differ so much in physical attributes and behavior, I choose to refer to them as being either secondary or primary group members.

Secondary group members are males that achieved group membership only within the last year and are usually two and a half years old, but such groups could include one-and-a-half-year-old bucks that dispersed from their natal range when 12 months old, as well as three-and-a-half-year old males who delayed dispersing. Secondary group members tend to be superior to Class 2 bucks in body size and antler development, but still not fully grown themselves, they are submissive to older bucks. Secondary group members' antlers are normally branched (most have eight points) and larger than those of most younger bucks, but are rarely equal in size to those of older individuals.

Because these secondary group members are so psychologically suppressed by older bucks, they exhibit

True fraternal groups usually number less than six individuals. In summer, however, bucks from neighboring groups may intermingle to form larger, if temporary, male associations.

Low-level threats and aggressive actions prior to the rut establish each male's identity and social standing, thus diminishing the likelihood of more hostile encounters during the breeding season.

low testosterone levels, do minimal scent-marking, are normally quite inactive during the rut, tend to carry their antlers longer than any other bucks (at least on northern range), and undergo minimal rut season weight loss. In a structured male society, they are readily identifiable during the rut based upon their fairly nice antlers but lack of neck swelling (the result of low testosterone). They have almost no opportunity to breed in a socially structured population.

Most primary fraternal group members will be three and a half or four and a half years old. In high density deer herds, some could be older and difficult to distinguish from the alpha (Class 4) bucks. Although they will have achieved their full skeletal size, their body weight, rut season neck measurements, and antler size are likely to increase in subsequent years.

Within a fraternal group, pairs of bucks in this subclass tend to develop close social bonds and can generally be found together during the summer months. They may even begin to wander out of their normal summer range together on brief exploratory jaunts.

Members of fraternal groups readily engage in ritualized sparring matches that eventually lead to a strict dominance hierarchy in advance of the breeding season. However, primary members become extremely hormonally charged, aggressive, and totally unpredictable during the breeding season. They are physiologically and psychologically well equipped in all aspects of ritualized breeding behavior, are likely to make as many antler rubs and scrapes as older alpha bucks, and compete readily, but cautiously, for breeding privileges. Especially when the "breeding window" is quite narrow, as it is on northern deer range where most does breed only during a few weeks in November, primary fraternal group bucks probably do considerable breeding, but only when the alpha buck is not available.

Whenever violent buck fights erupt, primary fraternal group bucks are probably involved, less frequently with alpha males but more commonly with primary members from neighboring fraternal groups. Winners of such battles become psychologically "high" and physiologically stimulated. If their physical attributes match their psyche, they are probably on their way to assuming the prominent role of "dominant floaters" (Class 4) in the years ahead; if not, the next battle may lead to their demise.

We generally assume that all sexually mature bucks compete to breed as many does as possible during each rut. But Dr. Valerius Geist suggests some mature bucks badly beaten while fighting opt not to compete for breeding privileges, at least for that season, do not socialize with other large bucks, and live a solitary life.

An alpha male—animals such as these, the largest and most dominant bucks in whitetail populations, rule male societies and, as herd sires, perform the majority of the breeding.

Geist suggests, "The opting-out strategy works when there is a die-off, as can happen in a severe winter. When the large bucks, exhausted by the rut, may die, he [the mature buck who has opted out of the year's breeding cycle] is more likely to survive, having spent the fall feeding and resting. Not only does opting out preserve the buck's fat reserves, which he may then draw on to survive lean times, but it also gives him a head start for growth the following spring and summer. This in turn increases his chances for survival and his ultimate body size and thus his ability to fight during the next rut. Moreover, following a population crash and the concomitant decline in sexual competition, a huge master buck may now breed a greater number of females. That buck thereby increases his genes proportionately in the herd."

Class 4 Males: Dominant Floaters. Dominant floaters — a term most aptly coined by Brown — are the alpha bucks. They are the most dominant males in the population and the true social governors of the male society.

In a socially balanced whitetail population, most alpha males are five and a half to nine and a half years old, fully grown and mature in all respects. Typically they are superb physical specimens — the largest-bodied, largest-antlered, and most physically fit male examples of the species. They possess highly polished competitive skills gained through years of experience in sparring, and in fighting when necessary.

Most importantly, dominant floaters exhibit finely tuned ritualized threat patterns and dominance displays as well as elaborate signposting and courtship behavior. Such talents frequently enable them to bluff and intimidate younger bucks, thereby eliminating the need to physically prove their superiority and run the risk of injury. They are masterful scent-markers.

Beginning in late summer, dominant bucks tend to be wide-ranging travelers. They move freely, "floating" uncontested over a relatively large breeding range occupied by several fraternal groups, members of which the alpha male dominates through stereotyped threat patterns and frequent scent-marking of overhead tree branches. During autumn, dominant floaters are masters at producing numerous strategically located antler rubs and pawed ground scrapes to advertise and commu-nicate their superior social rank and presence to other bucks as well as does. These scent-marked signposts carry the maker's distinctive odor and special pheromones, which convey long-lasting messages and have strong suppressor effects upon younger bucks while being highly attractive to estrous females.

The longevity of a dominant floater will depend upon many factors but hinges heavily upon his general health status and the amount of competition he receives from up-and-coming bucks. Should he become injured, show any weakness, or falter in the least when attempting to reaffirm his supreme social rank, he will be challenged repeatedly by other bucks. As a result, he'll likely lose his high social standing, if not his life. I doubt if any buck can hold the alpha position beyond 10 and a half years of age when faced with competition from prime-age bucks.

Class 5 Males: Seniors. Seniors are aged bucks past their physical prime. Some may be as young as eight and a half or nine and a half years old, but most will be older. Obviously, few bucks ever achieve such an old age in hunted populations. I once calculated that less than one buck in 360,000 ever reached such an old age in heavily hunted Lower Michigan.

In some ungulate species, senior males reportedly retreat from society, no longer compete with other males for social rank or breeding opportunities, and live out their final years peaceably as hermits. Having observed whitetail bucks for many years, however, I find it difficult to believe that the alpha whitetail buck relinquishes his supreme status so graciously. Generally, those bucks that struggle unsuccessfully to hold their high dominance rank enter winter in wretched physical condition and perish before winter's end. Others may

A mature whitetail buck with its polished antlers and rut-swollen neck
is one of the most impressive sights in nature.

not even survive the onslaught of competition from younger bucks during the rut period.

Some senior whitetail bucks do manage to survive, for a few years at any rate, where the climate is not so severe, but they show their old age: They are gray-faced and not nearly as firm and well-rounded as are prime-age bucks during the pre-rut period. Senior bucks also exhibit decreased testosterone secretion and more likely grow degenerate (stunted) and malformed antlers.

The oldest free-ranging buck I know of was 17 years old when it was live-captured in northern Minnesota. Few bucks live beyond 12 and a half years, however, as most such aged individuals suffer from arthritis, have badly worn teeth, and normally succumb to malnutrition or predation during the winter season.

OVERVIEW

In my view, the whitetail female society evolved primarily to maximize reproductive success, even in the presence of effective predators, and as a way of making efficient use of food and cover resources, which probably changed suddenly and frequently during primeval times. Fires, floods, windstorms, and similar calamities no doubt periodically devastated mature forests, set back vegetation succession, and produced patches of ideal habitat for whitetails. It is my belief that the female whitetails' social system evolved to cope with such environmental change, to allow the species to take quick advantage of these chance opportunities.

Compared to that of the female, a male's climb on the social ladder is a much more prolonged and tenuous struggle. For one thing, it takes a male longer — about six years — to reach his maximum body size. Also, in an age-structured male society — as such organization likely evolved naturally in whitetail populations — the immature buck first serves as an obedient subordinate in an apprenticeship role wherein he grows, learns, and matures in all aspects. Each subsequent autumn he is somewhat larger, stronger, and has larger antlers. He's a little wiser too. He advances accordingly, gradually gaining social status from one year to the next as he matures and rises in dominance over his peers.

It should be understood, of coarse, that the whitetail societal sketch I present here is for a well nourished and rapidly expanding northern deer herd living in forested habitat. Obviously, deer populations living in a different climate or habitat, those greatly distorted by human-induced mortality, or those that are extremely malnourished probably respond differently.

Nonetheless, the system I describe probably operates in most natural environments when habitat conditions are favorable and whitetail populations are growing

Though members of the same species, the doe and buck whitetail have evolved separate social strategies that ultimately determine which individuals will perpetuate their genes in future whitetail populations.

rapidly. Regardless of the environment, however, most adult females eventually breed, and it is largely the female's reproductive success and longevity that determines her rate of social growth and, ultimately, the hereditary intricacy of the female society.

By comparison, the whitetail buck's social life is more complex. Physical size and strength, in addition to longevity, become important factors in determining his breeding success. In a natural population, few whitetail bucks achieve the pinnacle role of herd sires.

With flourishing whitetail populations, highly structured female societies are not uncommon in many sections of the country, primarily because female deer tend to be lightly hunted. However, since antlered deer are heavily harvested in most areas, few hunted deer populations exhibit highly structured male social organization as I've outlined here. Instead, in most areas, the annual harvest of bucks is so excessive that yearling (Class 2) bucks must prematurely assume herd sire roles and do most of the breeding. In the absence of mature bucks — the social governors — the rut becomes a chaotic scramble among young bucks to breed any estrous doe, thereby minimizing the opportunity for selective mating and decreasing the tendency to perpetuate adaptive traits.

In healthy, balanced whitetail populations, most does will be bred by older, dominant males; in populations where larger males have been removed from the population, subdominant males, such as the one pictured above, perform most of the breeding.

SUMMERTIME SCENT-MARKING

Whitetails have superhuman, or "macrosmatic," olfactory capabilities, meaning they are able, far beyond our weak human powers of odor detection, to recognize faint traces of scent. Deer use their noses to test for small, volatile airborne molecules and possess a specialized vomeronasal system to analyze larger, less volatile molecules that exist in solution in some liquids, such as urine. They use their superior sense of smell to locate nourishing food and water and to avoid predators. And they employ those magical powers, in conjunction with glandular secretions and body odors — referred to as chemical signals — as their primary means of communication throughout the year. (According to University of Georgia researcher Karl Miller, "Chemical signals that relay information among animals are called pheromones. This term was originally coined to describe chemical sex attractants in insects, but has since been expanded to include any chemical produced by one individual that transfers information to

How whitetails transmit, receive, and interpret chemical signals is still something of an enigma to researchers. Scent communications are known, however, to serve a variety of purposes such as indicating sexual status, personal identity, and dominance.

another member of the same species; some researchers reserve 'pheromones' for insects and use 'chemical signals' when referring to mammals.")

To a forest-dwelling animal like the whitetail, which lives in dense cover, chemical signals are much more important in communication than are visual signs and vocalizations that serve only immediate, short-range purposes. Body odors left on objects in the environment identify the maker and permit scent-matching of marks with individuals. These odors produce long-lasting messages that remain functional in the maker's absence and can be memorized by other deer.

Communicative odors produced by deer may include secretions from skin glands, urine, vaginal secretions and, probably, saliva. Feces also serve as a means of odor communication in some animals, and might in whitetails, too, but this has not been documented.

Investigators have identified seven types of skin glands in white-tailed deer that likely play some role in scent communication. These include the forehead, preorbital, and nasal glands, located on the head; the tarsal, metatarsal, and interdigital glands, found on the legs, and the preputial gland on the buck's penis sheath. More glands undoubtedly exist.

There are many mysteries surrounding whitetails' use of scent in communicating matters of social significance,

and the secretions they use, the way they present them, and the messages they convey change with the seasons.

MOTHERS AND YOUNG

It is important for the whitetail mother to learn the identity of her offspring as soon as possible — a process probably totally dependent upon odor. She learns the odors of her young soon after birth, when she licks them free of embryonic membranes and fluids, and then grooms each fawn's anal-genital area.

Although this critical period varies between species, a whitetail mother probably learns the odor of her offspring within a few hours. Despite the fawns' sedentary nature and frequent self-grooming, which tend to minimize odors, even young fawns have some odors. In subsequent visits to her young, who remain out of sight in dense vegetation, then, the mother will smell her offspring before allowing them to suckle and will reject fawns other than her own.

Aside from odors produced in association with estrus, namely vaginal secretions, the use of chemical signals and scent-marking by female whitetails is poorly understood. Related does share ancestral range during most of the year. However, they tend to occupy and defend individual adjacent territories from incursions by other does during the early stages of fawn rearing. Therefore, female deer

Whitetail mothers learn to recognize their offspring by odor, a process that takes place immediately after birth, when the doe licks her fawn clean of embryonic fluids and then grooms it.

Chemical signals deposited by deer on overhanging branches may serve to delineate territorial boundaries at certain times of the year, but the chemicals they secrete may communicate entirely different messages at other times.

must employ some form of marking to delineate individual areas of occupation, and thus reduce stress from territorial incursions by female clan members.

It requires several days before the newborn fawn imprints upon its mother. It is interesting to note, however, that within a relatively short time the fawn will then learn the boundaries of its mother's territory. Even without guidance, a two- to three-week-old fawn will flee from a predator, but the fawn will not leave its mother's fawn-rearing range. How the youngster can determine the boundaries of the area, which might cover 20 or more acres of heavily forested land, is unclear, but maternal odors probably play an important role.

Noted researcher Karl Miller considers the tarsal glands, located hock-high on the inside of the hind legs, as the most important source of chemical information for deer. According to Miller, "Whitetails obtain information on individual identity, dominance position, physical condition, and reproductive status from odors arising from this gland. The tarsal of females appears to be used primarily for individual identification. Does frequently sniff the tarsals of others in their social group, and fawns use this scent to identify their mothers."

Certain sebaceous and sudoriferous glands underlay the tarsal gland, but urine is probably the primary

*If a doe and her fawn have been separated, as they are during the
hours when the fawn remains in hiding between nursing periods, the
mother will first confirm her fawn's identity before allowing it to suckle.*

Bucks are particularly fond of leaving chemical signals on overhead branches. These signals, among other functions, probably communicate a buck's identity, in the form of a chemical calling card, that conveys the animal's dominance.

source of chemical signals produced by the tarsal. Miller suggests: "The enlarged sebaceous glands underlying the tarsal tuft secrete a fatty material that adheres to the tarsal hairs. During a behavior called rub-urination, deer urinate on their tarsal hairs (while simultaneously rubbing them together). The fatty material then selectively retains fat-soluble compounds from the urine." Researchers speculate that differences in the composition of these volatile compounds produce distinctive odors that identify the individual — allowing the doe to "speak" through her urine.

While following tame deer, Timothy Sawyer determined that does rub-urinated 1.2 times daily and urinated in a normal posture eight to ten times each day. Given the doe's high frequency of marking via urine, she must leave a host of socially important messages that clearly delineate her movements and range occupation.

BUCKS

During the breeding season, bucks produce highly visible signposts, in the form of antler rubs and ground scrapes, to express dominance and attract prospective mates. This scent-marking is accompanied by rather violent aggressive action: Bucks use their antlers to rub the bark from trees, to thrash brush, and to break overhead limbs while depositing scent, and they paw the ground like irate bulls.

Whitetail bucks scent-mark at other times of the year too, but do so in a nonaggressive manner. Bucks judiciously scent-mark overhead branches on their summer range. When carrying velvet antlers, however, they may deposit social odors so subtly that most marking goes completely unnoticed, at least to the comparatively dull human senses. Heavily marked twigs acquire an oily or greased appearance, and deer hairs can often be found adhered to the tips of a frayed branch. Therefore, observations indicate that not only the manner in which bucks scent-mark branches changes seasonally, they also suggest that the substances deposited and messages conveyed while marking might differ throughout the year.

In reviewing study findings, Miller summarizes the whitetail buck's complex scraping behavior this way: "Although frequencies of overhead branch marking tended to be higher for dominants than for sub-ordinates, it occurred frequently among all bucks throughout the year. A scrape sequence is a composite of three separate behavior patterns that also occur inde-pendently of each other, suggesting that scrapes have multiple functions. Perhaps the overhanging branch con-veys individual identity and presence, pawing denotes aggressive intent to other bucks, and urine deposited in the scrape may relay social or physiological status to bucks and does." Miller cautions, however, ". . . sources of scent deposited on the overhanging branch (during any time of year) are highly speculative."

On northern range, where whitetails vacate their summering grounds and migrate long distances to wintering areas, bucks intensively scent-mark overhead branches on their traditional summer range as soon as they return in spring. Sometimes they even complete the full scrape sequence by pawing the ground and urinating at the site. It is my belief that such marking helps bucks reclaim familiar habitat that has been devoid of deer for several months. Buck marking in spring might also intimidate does, forcing them to seek other areas for fawn rearing.

In my enclosure studies, bucks occupied and scent-marked very small ranges — generally less than 200 acres in size — during May and June, the period of maximum antler growth. Nutritious forage was then very abundant, probably requiring minimal travel for bucks to secure a daily supply of forage. But rapidly growing antlers are also fragile during this period, which probably causes bucks to be more cautious and sedentary in order to minimize velvet antler damage. In late July, however, when their antler growth was nearly completed and their antler cores began to mineralize, some of the enclosure bucks wandered into adjacent doe-occupied ranges where they also scent-marked overhead branches.

These observations further indicate that the distribution of bucks and the location of their scent-marks changes as the summer season progresses. Even the secretions, messages, and audience may change from one month to the next.

Clearly, adult bucks are the primary "markers" and "readers" of social messages attached to overhead branches during summer. But specifically what marking ingredients are used, when they are used, and where they come from are highly debatable.

When marking branches, most of which are about head-high, a buck "mouths" the branch tips, rubs them with his forehead, preorbital area, nose, antlers, and chin, while pausing periodically to sniff and lick the branches. It's as if the entire process involved some highly sophisticated signal code.

Bucks place scent on overhead branches (sometimes when standing on their hind legs) with their heads, primarily for the benefit of other bucks; it is uncertain, however, whether those secretions are actually produced on the head or the buck merely uses his head to transfer secretions from other parts of his body to branches.

Two types of glands are most often responsible for producing chemical signals: sebaceous glands and sudoriferous glands. Both types are found over the skin surface but are concentrated in certain areas and undergo seasonal changes in activation and function.

Forehead glands of whitetail bucks are known to produce pheromones that express dominance. All deer possess these glands, but the most active glands are found on dominant bucks during the rut. When bucks rub shrubs and trees with their antlers and forehead, they create signposts that are visually noticeable and carry the maker's odor, signaling presence of a dominant animal.

Because of their obvious behavioral importance, it's tempting to credit the forehead glands as the primary source of secretions transferred to branch tips on a year-round basis. However, histological examination of the forehead skin reveals that glands in this area are quite inactive while bucks carry velvet antlers. Increased secretion from the forehead glands does not occur until the antlers harden and velvet is shed. Also, use of these secretions is normally associated with agonistic, threatening behavior, whereas summertime scent communication among bucks is more informative and less agonistic.

It seems illogical that bucks would use the same secretions to present both friendly information, such as

*In whitetail populations, scent marking is primarily used to convey
messages between adult males. Here, a buck in the process of shedding
its antler velvet "reads" a chemical message left on a rub made by
another male.*

When marking overhead branches, as well as chewing the tender tips of the branches, bucks may rub their antlers and forehead glands on the vegetation, leaving behind a variety of glandular substances.

identity and presence, as well as aggressive information concerning dominance and social rank. If secretions from forehead glands are the primary source of odor used in marking overhead limbs, then other changes in body chemistry, mixing of secretions, and different behaviorisms must be involved in producing messages that change with the whitetail's reproductive status.

Other potential sources of overhead branch marking substances are the preorbital glands (also referred to as the antorbital or lachrymal gland), located immediately in front of the eye, and the nasal sebaceous glands found inside the nostril. In some ungulate species, such as the Thomson's gazelle, the preorbital gland produces an oily strong-smelling substance believed to carry pheromones used for marking territorial boundaries. In whitetails, this gland is a sac-like structure generally filled with dead skin cells and foreign matter. Although whitetail bucks seem to use this gland in scent-marking, researchers are uncertain if it produces socially important scent.

Nasal glands have been found in a number of deer species, including whitetails, but their function is unknown. Originally, investigators postulated that materials from this gland were atomized during snorting behavior. That idea has been abandoned, though, because the gland has since been found to produce a fatty, lipid material of low volatility. Still, this does not preclude the possibility that such fatty substances serve as a carrier for other scents.

Velvet antlers are also well endowed with sebaceous glands, which produce an oily substance called sebum. Sebum helps to grease the surface of the antler, making it slippery and resistant to abrasion or injury. According to the late Anthony Bubenik, bucks smear sebum produced by the velvet over their bodies, then onto vegetation at head-height, "leaving a strong scent track."

Bubenik proposed that hardened antlers also play a primary role in scent communication during the rut. He suggested that some species purposely "perfume" their antlers by urinating on them, rubbing them on certain glands, or thrashing them in urine-soaked wallows.

Even mature whitetail bucks may, on occasion, rub their antlers in urine-marked scrapes or on their bodies. However, aside from the fact that subordinate deer sometimes sniff a dominant's antlers, I know of no firm data supporting the claim that deer antlers either produce or are used to carry chemical signals.

Odors emanating from the tarsal tuft apparently allow deer of both sexes to transmit a wealth of socially important information. All deer exhibit the behaviorism referred to as rub-urination, wherein they urinate over their tarsal tufts while rubbing them together. Although does normally lick the excess urine from their tarsals,

mature bucks are less likely to do so, especially during the rut. It is the bacterial action of urine trapped on the tarsal hairs that produces the buck's characteristic musky odor.

Dominant bucks tend to rub-urinate into their scrapes. Some investigators propose that bucks also rub their urine-charged tarsals with their snout, then transfer the odors to overhead branches — another very plausible theory without supporting evidence.

Saliva is a potentially potent but very poorly understood substance involved in chemical signaling among many species. In the boar, for example, certain steroids (androstenol and androsternone) produced by the salivary glands act as pheromones that play an important role in courtship. There is also evidence of sex differences in the morphology of salivary glands in some species. Some observers suggest that saliva, when used directly or applied to the coat while self-grooming or grooming others, may function as a prime source of socially important odors among many mammals.

Whitetail bucks salivate profusely during the rut. This habit, in addition to their striking behavior of licking overhead branches year round, suggests they use saliva as a marking ingredient. Saliva may be a prime source of socially important odors for deer when applied directly to overhead branches, alone or in combination with other glandular secretions, or when first applied to the coat and mixed with other substances while grooming. Unfortunately, researchers know preciously little about such things.

THE SOCIAL ROLE

Even Charles Darwin recognized that scent communication among mammals, especially as it relates to reproduction and other matters of social significance, is highly dependent upon the achievement of adulthood. Sebaceous gland development depends upon sex hormones produced by the testes, ovaries, or adrenal glands, which are minimally funcional prior to the achievement of puberty.

In our quest to understand chemical communication in white-tailed deer, it's tempting to search for simple answers and simple chemical compounds — as in the case of insect pheromones. It is important to recognize, however, that deer have a rather complex

social system that is dependent upon a complex communication system. White-tailed deer seem to have the capacity to send out a wide array of chemical signals, which presumably convey an equally wide array of messages, in order to satisfy their social needs. Having the ability to alter the proportion of certain ingredients, combine secretions, or hold and age them if necessary provides for a complexity of odor signals. When combined with different methods of presenting this multitude of odors, the chemical language of whitetails must be immense.

Until we more fully understand white-tailed deer social organization, we will have difficulty in determining how they use chemical signals to "talk" to one another and precisely what silent messages are being conveyed.

Scent communications takes place between and among deer of all ages and both sexes. The entire repertoire of signals used by deer is no doubt as immense as it is complicated.

FAWN DEVELOPMENT

As with most prey species, the most precarious and dangerous time in the life of a white-tailed deer is during its first few weeks of life. The ungainly newborn fawn spends most of its time in hiding, is highly dependent upon maternal care, and is very vulnerable to predators. In order to survive the dangers of early life, the young fawn must grow rapidly and become strong enough to run from predators as soon as possible. In fact, the rapid growth rate of young whitetails and their ability to run surprisingly well by two weeks of age are adaptations that likely evolved in response to the threat imposed by predators. Poor maternal nutrition, disease, certain nutritional deficiencies, or other stress factors that slow fawn body growth tend to slow other physiological changes that are necessary to accommodate increasing energy demands. As a result, fawns that grow slowly also have less endurance, are more susceptible to diseases, suffer more from parasitism, and remain vulnerable to predation longer than usual. Wolves,

Until it is old enough to escape predators on its own, a whitetail fawn is extremely vulnerable. Until then, staying close to its protective mother is the fawn's best defense.

coyotes, and bears can capture and kill even large healthy fawns, given the right conditions, but study evidence indicates these predators generally end up killing the lighter, weaker fawns.

Another adaptation favoring whitetail survival is the animal's timing of its reproductive cycle: Does are geared to giving birth during late spring and early summer, when lush vegetation provides excellent hiding cover for fawns. New plant growth also provides an abundant supply of nutritious forage necessary if the lactating doe is to produce a maximum amount of nourishing milk. The young fawns also need nutritious vegetation to supplement their milk diet.

During summer, generally within a three-month period, young-of-the-year whitetails change from frail suckling infants solely dependent upon their mothers' milk for sustenance to robust, metabolically weaned ruminants. Although the growth and behavioral development of whitetail fawns are continuous, researchers at Cornell

University suggest the whitetail fawn's suckling stage can be divided into the seclusion phase, transitional phase, and juvenile ruminant phase. Logically, depending upon their birth date and level of nutrition, some fawns develop more rapidly than others.

Progressing northward over whitetails' geographic range, a greater percentage of the fawns are born during a relatively brief period in late May and early June. By early summer, most of these northern fawns will have already advanced beyond the cryptic hiding stage. Then, having become strong enough to run from predators, they will assume more active and more sociable lifestyles. In some areas, however, many fawns will be born late, during early to midsummer, and lag behind others in size and behavioral development.

LATE-BORN FAWNS

In the rich farmlands of the Midwest, where deer live at fairly low densities and enjoy excellent nutrition year

Lush vegetation is important to fawns, as a source of food as well as for the protective hiding cover it provides them.

round, a high percentage of one-year-old does will produce their first fawns. Since these precocious doe fawns breed (when six to nine months old) about a month later than adult does, their fawns usually are born in July or August, about a month later than fawns of older does.

Although about half of the doe fawns in southern Michigan's farmbelt usually breed, less than five percent breed in heavily forested Upper Michigan. In the George Reserve enclosure located in southern Michigan, for example, Dale McCullough found that one-year-old females produced a significant number of the annual newborn when deer density was low, but did not breed at high densities. McCullough observed doe fawns breeding only at low population density, when deer enjoyed exceptionally good nutrition and virtually all of the newborn fawns survived.

In order to achieve puberty and breed, a doe fawn must attain a certain critical fat-lean body mass, but numerous factors seem to be involved. In northern climes, natural selection has minimized poorly timed births (those being too early or too late), where nutritional constraints brought on by inclement weather during autumn probably serve to curtail physical development among young deer. Hence, few female fawns on northern range achieve the optimal body size

This pregnant doe is still carrying her fawn in early summer. Compared to fawns born in late spring, her late-born youngster will lag behind in physical development, a distinct disadvantage.

During its first few weeks of life, a fawn's cryptic coloration and seclusive habits are its chief defenses against predators.

and fatness necessary for breeding, resulting in their low fertility rate and a low incidence of late-born fawns.

Late-born fawns are most prevalent in southern environments, where unbred adult does might re-cycle and come into estrus as often as seven times during one season. Furthermore, many southern states have very long hunting seasons in which bucks are preferentially harvested, skewing adult sex ratios heavily in favor of females prior to peak breeding. Then, because adult males are in short supply, many females do not mate during their first estrus period. Instead, they breed during subsequent heat cycles, later in the rut, and do not give birth until one to several months later than usual.

THE SECLUSION PHASE

The seclusion phase for whitetails is from birth to 10 days of age, when fawns normally weigh less than 11 pounds. During this period a fawn spends about 92 percent of its time lying in seclusion, relying upon its inactivity and camouflaged speckled coat as its chief defenses against predators. Instead of fleeing from predators, the fawn will crouch and hide, sometimes exhibiting depressed breathing and a slowed heart rate referred to as "alarm bradycardia." This seclusion phase of development also allows the young fawn to shunt most of the nutrients it consumes into body growth, instead of wasting energy on extraneous activity that might also draw the attention of predators.

The gestation period for white-tailed deer averages about 200 days, but it tends to be a few days longer when mothers are malnourished during pregnancy. Healthy newborn fawns weigh about six to eight pounds at birth. Some may weigh as much as 12 pounds, but those born to malnourished mothers may weigh as little as two pounds. Fawns weighing less than five pounds at birth generally die shortly after parturition because they are too weak to stand and nurse, are abandoned, or their mothers produce no milk.

As a rule, single fawns average about a half pound heavier at birth than one of a pair of twins. This divergence in weight tends to widen among litters born to malnourished does. This physiological tendency sometimes allows one fawn to survive at the expense of the other, when the probability that both can survive is unlikely. When a doe reaches a crucial low level of nutrition, however, such disparity is less evident, and both fetuses are generally doomed.

Despite their smaller body size and tendency to give birth about a month later than adult does, healthy one-year-old does tend to produce sizable offspring. Studies conducted at the Cusino Wildlife Research Station suggested that late-fawning young does may be in a different physiological state during the latter part of pregnancy than are adult does that fawn earlier. That is, production of growth hormones and prolactin, which peak during summer, may contribute to exceptional growth of fetuses carried by late breeding doe fawns, resulting in larger fawns at birth.

Deer milk is higher in fat, protein, dry matter, and energy content than milk produced by domestic ruminants. The doe's diet has little or no influence upon the composition or quality of her milk, but poor nutrition may cause her to produce less milk than normal. Or, if the doe is seriously malnourished, she might produce no milk at all. Young fawns generally nurse only two or three times daily, consuming about eight ounces of milk per meal. Given their mother's good health and a plentiful supply of nutritious milk, fawns gain nearly a half pound in body weight per day during early life.

When less than 10 days old, sibling fawns bed separately, and almost all of a fawn's activity, which is initiated by the mother when she seeks out the hidden fawn, centers around nursing and grooming. Bouts of activity generally last for 10 to 30 minutes and occur once or twice during daytime and once, or not at all, at night. Since important predators like the coyote and gray wolf hunt mostly at night, daytime activity is considered to be an anti-predator adaptation.

Predation by coyotes, wolves, bobcats, bears, and wild dogs accounts for the majority of fawn losses during the youngsters' early stages of development.

Her offspring in hiding, a doe must stay some distance away from the fawn, to avoid drawing the attention of predators, but she must remain close enough to come to its defense if need be.

The success of the whitetail fawn's hiding strategy also depends on the mother staying an optimal distance away from her hidden fawns. The mother must stay far enough away to minimize drawing attention to her fawns, but be close enough to defend them when necessary. Some studies also show that, over the first four weeks of their fawns' lives, mothers stay closer to their young during the night than during the day.

Despite the young fawn's inactivity, the healthy individual is capable of traveling a quarter of a mile or so, if necessary, when only a few days old. If seriously threatened by predators, for example, the mother may lead the fawn to a hiding place beyond the boundaries of her fawn-rearing area. In doing so, the mother must maintain a moderate speed at which the fawn can travel. She will also display a crouched (tail down) body posture that tends to elicit the fawn's "heeling" response, and encourage the fawn to follow her by emitting soft mewing vocalizations. Usually, however, a fawn occupies a range of 10 to 20 acres in size during the seclusion phase, and its mother leads it less than 500 feet from one bed site to the next.

THE TRANSITIONAL PHASE

When fawns are 10 to 50 days old and weigh roughly 11 to 33 pounds, they are considered to be in a tran-sitional stage of development. This is when they become strong enough to run from predators and increase the number and length of their daily activity bouts. (A 10-day-old fawn can outrun a man, and a 15-day-old fawn is very difficult for any natural predator to catch.)

Transitional phase fawns are active about 20 percent of the time, more frequently accompany their mothers, and start consuming more vegetation.

Provided the doe's milk supply is adequate, fawns undersized at birth tend to exhibit accelerated weight gain; by one month of age there seems to be little weight difference among well-fed fawns, regardless of their birth weights.

Young fawns are very efficient in converting nutrients into skeletal and muscle growth, but they lay down minimal fat until they are weaned. The average fawn may double its birth weight within two weeks and triple it within one month. Although average birth weights for males and females are almost identical, males generally outweigh females by about one-half pound at one month of age. If maternal nutrition is poor, however, and the doe's milk supply is limited, fawns undersized at birth will also be undersized at weaning age.

Fawns two to three weeks old nibble some vegetation but cannot survive without their mothers' milk; the rumen-reticulum portions of a fawn's four-chambered

*In their first weeks of life, sibling fawns bed separately, which helps
ensure that at least one will live if the other is discovered and killed by
a predator. Later, when they've grown strong enough to flee from
predators, the fawns bed together.*

stomach are not yet developed sufficiently to handle the chores of rumination. But the capacity and function of the rumen-reticulum increases as the fawn gains weight. When fawns are five to six weeks of age and weigh about 25 pounds, their forage intake and nighttime activity increase substantially. Fawns older than this can compensate for decreased milk intake by eating more vegetation, and they can survive without milk if absolutely necessary.

Siblings bed separately until they are 18 to 32 days old. Thereafter they normally bed together more than 70 percent of the time. What motivates siblings to suddenly unite is unknown. Such union seems to depend primarily upon the fawns' rate of physical and behavioral development and their ability to flee from predators.

After about one month of age, fawns more frequently initiate independent bouts of activity. They also become more visible at this time, and those that are in subpar health because of poor maternal

nutrition, disease, or heavy parasitism become increasingly vulnerable to predation. For example, in the Midwest, young fawns are reasonably safe while hidden in dense vegetation, but slow, sickly animals from four to seven weeks old become conspicuous and easily picked off by marauding coyotes and domestic dogs.

THE JUVENILE RUMINANT PHASE

Whitetail fawns are considered to be in a juvenile ruminant phase when they are from 50 to 100 days old and weigh from 33 to 55 pounds. By the time fawns weigh 30 to 35 pounds, generally at about eight weeks of age, the rumen-reticulum portions of their stomachs achieve nearly adult proportions. Fawns at this stage of development are active about half of the time and devote a large portion of their active time to foraging. Some researchers propose that the role of milk production and nursing after a fawn achieves this age and size may be less

After two to three months, fawns spend less time in hiding and nurse less often. They now begin traveling with their mothers and begin consuming vegetation as their major source of sustenance.

important to the fawn's nutritional benefit than it is to maintaining female-fawn social contact.

Fawns older than eight weeks graze regularly. They actively forage about 16 percent of the time and lie down and ruminate nearly an equal amount. Fawns this age typically feed with their mother before bedding, rest for a while, then seek out their mother again. Fawns spend less time in hiding and start to accompany their mothers when four to six weeks old. After eight weeks, they will spend more than half of their time traveling, feeding, and bedding with their mothers. As a result, the fawn's daily rhythm of activity soon becomes more like that of an adult deer, with prominent peaks of activity occurring at sunrise, midday, sunset, and once or twice at night.

Concurrent changes occur in a young fawn's physiology along with its rapid gain in body size. During its second and third months, a fawn's resting metabolic rate, red blood cell counts, and hemoglobin concentrations rise, while its mean corpuscular volume decreases. These changes in blood chemistry allow for a more efficient exchange of oxygen and carbon dioxide and maximize the oxygen-carrying capacity of the blood. These changes are necessary to accommodate the young fawn's elevated oxygen requirements associated with greatly increased activity.

Fawns only a week or two old exhibit some play behavior, but such frolicking becomes more pronounced when they are a month or two old. Initially, fawns dash away from their mother, but only as far as 50 feet or so, then rush back again. Fawns one to two months old may run as far as 300 feet from their mother, often zigzagging, dodging, and bucking as they run. Twin fawns may chase one another, often circling and sometimes rearing on their hind legs and striking at one another in mock combat.

Researcher David Hirth notes that fawns play only in the presence of their mothers and always after nursing, not before. He suggests that the significance of play behavior by fawns is twofold: "First, it gives them practice in running and in eluding predators before they have a real need to do so. And second, the 'playful' nature of this activity makes it clear to nearby deer that this is just make-believe, an important message to get across for play involving bucking, kicking, and other forms of mock aggression."

During the fawns' first two months of life, social contacts are almost entirely restricted to associating with siblings and their mothers. During the third month, they gradually integrate into complex social groups. It was our experience in the Cusino enclosure investigations that newborn fawns are literally forced into

During fawns' first two months of life, they remain reclusive, associating only with siblings and with their mother. In their third month, fawns are gradually integrated into the mother's matriarchal group.

association with older sisters sooner than ordinary when deer density is high and many young does fail to rear fawns. Under such circumstances, the 10-week-old fawn may be found associating with an adult female relative almost as often as it does with its mother.

During late summer, when family groups of deer gather on open feeding areas, yearling does and adult does may exhibit play behavior with fawns, jumping and running in circles. Occasionally, especially on rich farmland in the Midwest, even adult bucks may engage in play behavior with does and fawns. Clearly, play behavior is a sign of good health — it probably only occurs among those deer that have excellent nutrition and excess energy.

As summer progresses and fawns become stronger and more sociable, their play behavior—bucking, jumping, and running—becomes more frequent. Often, fawns engage adult deer in their playful games.

SUMMER BEHAVIOR

Summer is usually a good time for white-tailed deer. It is a season when food and cover are about as plentiful as they'll be over most of the whitetail's range. It is then, too, that deer are most evenly distributed across their range. During summer, however, some environments are far better than others for deer, and, occasionally, wild fires, drought, or flooding may cause temporary depletion of vital resources in otherwise good deer habitat.

Like other wild animals, whitetails have four basic needs that must be supplied by the area in which they live: food, cover, water, and space. Obviously, many factors interact to determine the availability of these necessities, which, in some environments, vary greatly with the seasons. In the North, for example, deer must vacate vast areas of their summer range and migrate long distances to find areas of dense conifer cover that help buffer the cold and snow that accompany the harsh months of winter. In effect, northern deer have a distinct

In summer, bucks usually associate with other male whitetails and travel little. However, for reasons unknown, some bucks remain solitary and wander considerable distances.

summer range that is sometimes widely separated from their winter range. Southern deer, on the other hand, more likely live year round on the same area.

HOME RANGE

Whitetails show great fidelity to the areas in which they live most of their lives (referred to as their home range). Many factors, such as the animal's sex and age, the prevailing climate, dispersion of vegetative types, topography, and even ancestral habits will influence the location, size, and shape of a deer's home range.

Large unbroken tracts of pure deciduous or coniferous forest represent suboptimal habitats for whitetails, causing deer that use these habitats as home ranges to roam farther than usual. Summer home range size for deer in northern Minnesota, for example, may cover 120 to more than 1,000 acres. Likewise, deer in forested areas of New York reportedly have summer home ranges averaging nearly a square mile (640 acres) in size.

Yearling and older male whitetails generally travel over larger ranges than do females in all seasons. In landscapes where forest cover is severely fragmented and limited, adult males may travel extensive summer ranges of more than three square miles.

Given a good mix of food, cover, and water during summer, however, most deer occupy home ranges averaging less than one square mile in area. Many deer find adequate resources on areas only 100 to 200 acres in size. Typically, the more diversified the habitat and the richer the soils, the better the summer habitat for deer. The better the habitat, the more abundant and healthy the deer occupying it.

In heavily forested regions, disturbances such as fires and logging create habitat diversity — "patchiness" of food and cover — that improves summer habitat for deer. Fertile farmlands interspersed with brushy swales and patches of timber also offer choice habitat for whitetails. During summer, even intensively farmed lands, with their "corn forests," offer deer an excellent combination of food and cover that is unavailable during other seasons.

Compared to whitetails on northern range, deer living in the southern United States have relatively small (often less than 100 acres in size) home ranges. But even these comparatively sedentary southern deer exhibit shifts in their home ranges through time. As a consequence, note Larry Marchinton and Karl Miller, "A southern deer's lifetime range is substantially larger than its home range at any one point in time. The home range of such animals looks like an amoeba: It extends a little here, then a little there, and over time its shape and even location may change."

*Given adequate resources, most deer, such as this doe, will rarely travel
beyond the square-mile area comprising their home range.*

The availability of resources also influences the shape of the whitetails' home range. Some ranges may be circular in shape, if resources are close at hand, but most are elongated. "The extent of the elongation," according to Marchinton and Miller, "varies with quality of habitat. If the habitat uniformly provides a good mix of essentials, or if the deer relies on only one type of vegetation, the oval is rather fat, and the deer ranges out in all directions from a central point to find what it needs. If the deer uses two or more types of vegetation, the oval is long and the deer's movements are more linear."

Deer density and social factors can also influence home range size. High deer density generally contributes to smaller home range sizes during early summer because the adult sexes tend to avoid one another, and does with fawns are still aggressive towards other deer. All deer become more sociable during late summer, however, as they intermingle and expand their ranges accordingly.

ACTIVITY PATTERNS

Whitetails are most active during late winter, early spring, and during the autumn breeding season. They exhibit a substantial decline in activity during summer. The high level of activity of deer in spring is due to their high metabolic demands following winter, a season of low forage quality and depletion of body fat. In spring, deer simply must spend more time foraging to meet their needs.

The decrease in deer activity during summer can be related to greatly improved nutritional conditions and an abundance of quality food close at hand. Despite the high energy demands associated with lactation among nursing does and antler growth among bucks, forage quality and quantity tend to exceed metabolic demands during summer; deer can literally fill up with nutritious foods while expending a minimal amount of activity.

Deer become increasingly active during late summer and early autumn as many forage plants mature, become more lignified, and decrease in nutritive value. At the same time, energy demands associated with growth, fattening, and breeding activity increase. The decrease in food quality, if not quantity, means that deer then must spend more time foraging to meet their metabolic requirements.

Whitetails are primarily crepuscular creatures: They are most active at dawn and dusk. However, they sometimes exhibit lesser peaks of activity at midday, when females are more active then males, and twice during the night. Typically, deer spend midday in heavy cover where they bed and chew their cud, rising only occasionally to shift bedding sites or to browse awhile.

As darkness approaches, they become more active and gravitate to open areas that provide better food sources but are generally unsafe during daylight. At night, they will alternately feed and bed in the open, then return to the safety of heavy cover just before sunrise.

Whitetails see very well at night and can detect even the slightest movement under any light intensity. They are well adapted for crepuscular and nocturnal behavior because of a membrane, the tapetum lucidum, located in the back of their eye. This membrane reflects light back through the receptor layer of the retina, brightening objects seen in dim light. It also accounts for the eye shine of deer seen when artificial lights are shone upon them at night.

Deer can also see well in bright light because of a ring of pigment that surrounds the cornea of their eye. The unique structure acts as an anti-glare device and is not found in other mammals that are strictly crepuscular or nocturnal.

According to Dietland Muller-Schwarze, professor of environmental biology at SUNY College of Environmental Science and Forestry in Syracuse, "Day or night, a deer's visual acuity is excellent. Under strong light, the pupils of the eye close into a slit, focusing light onto a horizontal band across the eye's retina. In exactly this streak are clustered the nerve cells that function as signal conductors, carrying messages from the photoreceptors to the brain. The arrangement and density of the nerve cells, called ganglion cells, in the visual streak account for the deer's ability to detect danger from afar."

Deer apparently have the proper photoreceptors, namely rods and cones, for color detection. Some experiments indicate that deer can discriminate colors (under laboratory conditions, at least), but not all studies agree that deer can distinguish colors in their natural environment. At best, deer probably rely upon their perception of only yellow and blue and are less sensitive to orange and red.

Whitetails are most active in the hours surrounding dawn and dusk. At night, they feed in open areas that would be dangerous to visit during daylight hours.

A whitetail's eyes are well adapted for night vision, yet the animal also sees quite well in bright light, due to a special pigment surrounding the corneas of its eyes.

Weather factors also influence deer activity. High summertime temperatures and strong winds, in particular, cause deer to become less active and restrict their movements to heavy cover. Deer seem especially edgy and are more inclined to lie low during high winds, when suspicious movements and sounds are all around and difficult to identify, and when swirling air currents hinder their ability to scent danger. For opposite reasons, deer are more active than usual during foggy weather, when their senses are especially keen.

ALARM SIGNALS

Whitetails employ a variety of visual and vocal signals to communicate danger to members of their social group. Young fawns, especially when hungry or threatened by predators, often "bleat" for attention from their mothers, but all deer might "bawl" loudly when injured or in the grasp of a predator.

Probably the most common alarm sound emitted by whitetails in response to danger is the "snort" — the sound that results when deer blow air through their nasal passages. Different types of snorts may be produced, depending upon the distance between the deer and the perceived source of danger. Snorts are also sometimes emitted during certain agonistic encounters, especially by a dominant animal as it lunges at its adversary.

When a deer is surprised at close range, it often gives a very short, almost explosive, blast of air through its nose and simultaneously runs away. Then the startled animal makes an all-out effort to escape as rapidly as possible. The associated noises, including reckless crashing through the underbrush and snorting, serve to alert other deer in the social group that danger is nearby. When danger is detected at a greater distance and the situation is obviously less life threatening, at least for the moment, deer will more often produce a series of longer snorts.

Studies conducted by David Hirth and Dale McCullough revealed that members of doe groups are much more likely to snort than are members of buck groups. Considering the evolutionary significance of alarm signals, the investigators hypothesized that snorting occurs more frequently in mother-young groups because these communications benefit related individuals. Unrelated bucks, on the other hand, are more likely to express "selfish behavior" by slipping away from danger quietly — thereby increasing their own fitness, at the expense of close competitors, for obtaining resources and mates.

"Tail flagging" combined with an easy bounding gait is a common visual alarm signal displayed by white-tailed deer in noncritical situations, as when a predator is detected at a distance. Bucks and does tend to flag

Flagging while they conspicuously bound away in escape is the primary visual signal used by deer to alert others of their species to the presence of danger.

Among ruminant prey such as deer, cud chewing is an effective anti-predation strategy. It allows deer to ingest food quickly, then regurgitate and chew it later in areas safe from marauding predators.

with about equal frequency when alarmed. When deer are surprised at close range, however, they neither bound nor flag; they simply dash away as rapidly as possible, holding their tails out straight.

Sometimes when an unidentifiable object is detected, a deer will stare at the object, cup its ears forward, and erect its tail to expose its white rump patch. This behavior is also used to alert other members of the group to potential danger. If the deer still cannot identify the object, it may stamp its forefeet in an attempt to make the potential predator move. If the object cannot be positively identified, the deer might bound away, tail flagging.

Miller and Marchinton emphasize that white-tailed deer have evolved an "on-again, off-again" rump patch. In most cases, whitetails rely upon their camouflage coloration to avoid predators, keeping their tail down to cover the conspicuous white area of the rump and underside of the tail. When discovered by predators, however, they tail flag — raising their tail to expose their white rump — to help maintain visual contact and the cohesiveness of the social group while fleeing.

FEEDING

Whitetails are ruminants and cud chewers. After swallowing their food, they regurgitate it to be chewed again—an eat now, chew later, highly adaptive anti-predation strategy.

Like all ruminants, whitetails also require fiber in their diet for normal rumen function. Unlike larger ruminants such as moose, elk, or domestic livestock, though, deer have considerably smaller rumen capacity and cannot digest highly fibrous or lignified foods. As a result, they must be more selective in their feeding habits, searching out and consuming the most nutritious and easily digested plants available. They must also feed more frequently.

Poorly digestible foods stay in a deer's stomach longer than usual, which decreases the animal's total consumption. Generally speaking, the more nutritious the food, the faster it passes through the digestive system. Obviously, the more food a deer can consume, the more nutrients it can assimilate, and the faster it will grow and gain body weight.

Good nutrition during late summer is especially critical for fawns. Fawns are generally weaned in August or early September, when 10 to 12 weeks old. Thereafter, they switch to eating vegetation. If they are to achieve maximum skeletal size and body weight prior to winter, they require nourishing forage that has from 14 to 22 percent protein content. By comparison, yearlings, which are also still growing, require 11 percent protein.

Mature whitetails require a diet that has from six to 10 percent protein, but the sexes exhibit subtle differences in food preferences. Adult bucks normally weight about 30 percent more than females and have a lower whole-body metabolic requirement per unit gut capacity. This difference presumably allows males to subsist on lower quality foods when nutritious ones become scarce. Females, however, seem unable to meet their energetic needs by filling up on less-nutritious foods, even when those foods are plentiful.

Soils in some parts of the country are of low fertility and, consequently, give rise to forage that is of low nutritive value for deer. If crude protein levels in deer forage fall below six percent, rumen function is seriously impaired. Deer then grow slowly, tend to exhibit delayed sexual maturity, and have poor reproductive success as compared to deer foraging on diets containing higher protein levels.

Wherever they live, deer are opportunistic feeders. They have distinct food preferences, but what they eat largely depends upon what is available. Consequently, as expected, the whitetail's diet changes as summer progresses, and it differs greatly from one region of the country to another.

Except where deer are overly abundant, whitetails usually find adequate nutrition from June through August. However, a large deer herd can drastically reduce or eliminate certain choice forage, which will adversely impact deer physical development. Also, prolonged hot weather and drought may "cure" the forage and make it less digestible.

In the Upper Great Lakes region and in the Northeast, green leafy browse becomes more important in the deer's summer diet as succulent herbaceous plant (forb) abundance decreases and grasses mature and dry. Initially, during early summer, deer forage heavily on forbs such as bracken fern, grasses, aster, hawkweed, goldenrod, dandelion, strawberry, and wild sarsaparilla.

Whitetails also feed most heavily upon aquatic plants during periods of low water levels in early summer. Depending upon availability, deer have been observed to selectively feed upon burreeds, filamentous algae, ribbonleaf pondweed, water horsetail, arrowhead, sedges, marsh cinquefoil, pond lily, and other aquatic plants. Such aquatic vegetation is fairly nutritious and a good source of sodium and other nutrients.

Aspen forests under 25 years of age are considered to be important summer habitats for deer throughout the Upper Great Lakes region. Although deer prefer leaves from aspen suckers less than one year old, aspen stands also yield other important summer deer foods such as maple, birch, willow, juneberry, hazel, cherry, strawberry,

Healthy whitetails reflect the quality of the environment in which they live. Where food sources are diverse and plentiful, robust whitetails prosper.

rose, honeysuckle, bush honeysuckle, and large-leaf aster. In Wisconsin, high utilization of aspen foliage was found to coincide with the period of the leaves' highest protein content (17 percent).

Fleshy fruits and mushrooms also supplement the diet of whitetails throughout their northern range. When available, fruits like blackberry, blueberry, huckleberry, plum, and crabapple are highly sought after.

Much to the dismay of farmers, deer throughout their range feed heavily upon certain agricultural crops during summer. In Illinois, Nixon and his coworkers reported that farm-produced crops provided nearly one-half of the whitetail's summer diet. Deer feed on corn silks during the pollination period in late June and early July, and on maturing corn in late summer. They also feed on soybean leaves from the time of germination until the plants stop growing in late August. Alfalfa, wheat, clover, and oats also are part of the farmland deer's diet.

In the Southeast, whitetail biologist Harry Jacobson reports summer deer foods are normally plentiful and include various broadleaf plants, browse species, mushrooms, and fruits such as blackberry, dewberry, and wild plum. He notes, however: "Late summer can bring seasonal stresses to deer in the Southeast if prolonged summer drought lowers the quality of plants and causes lignification. Then deer switch to less succulent browse foods such as greenbrier, gallberry, French mulberry, low-growing annual legumes, and less palatable herbaceous species."

Summer foods for whitetails in the Southwest include prickly pear, lechugilla, acacia, osage orange, grapes, sumac, oak, ash, and persimmon. Jacobson lists forbs like spurge, three-seeded mercuries, croton, Carolina snail-seed (or moonseed), chickweed, vetch, bush clovers, false indigo, and partridge pea as other common summer foods of whitetails throughout Texas and Oklahoma.

Among whitetails, fleshy fruits, including apples, are highly prized foods. In addition to wild fruits, deer also ingest a panoply of aquatic plants, forbs, herbs, and other foliage.

*In agricultural areas, deer take advantage of commercial crops and,
much to the dismay of farmers, readily graze on corn, soybeans, wheat,
clover, and oats.*

In the Southwest, whitetails have adapted to living on native vegetation such as prickly pear cactus, acacia brush, and osage orange.

However, drought can lead to serious food shortages and often poses a serious threat to the well-being of whitetails living in the Southwest. James Teer, director of the Welder Wildlife Foundation, believes rainfall quantity is one of the most important factors influencing whitetails in south-central Texas. "For the Llano Basin and Edwards Plateau whitetail populations," says Teer, "I believe that precipitation is the chief factor regulating range carrying capacity, and that deer population densities fluctuate about the carrying capacity in response to interaction of populations with their food supply. . . . Starvation was the primary cause of mortality during the drought. Many dead and dying (emaciated) deer were observed in drought years. In 1954 and 1956, hunters were reluctant to shoot emaciated deer, and total losses in those years were influenced accordingly. Many deer brought to check stations were considered unfit for the table."

Grazing pressure by domestic livestock generally increases the drought problem faced by whitetails in the Southwest. Instead of greatly reducing their herds, ranchers often strive to maintain their stock by feeding them supplements. Deer and livestock are then forced to compete for the same natural forages, because drought reduces the amount and kinds of forage available. Resultant competition between domestic livestock and deer is often serious and invariably leads to excessive starvation die-offs of deer.

Although water is an important component in the whitetail's diet, nutritionist Duane Ullrey explains that water requirements vary with climatic conditions, type of food, whitetails' physiological state (growth, maintenance, lactation), and amount of activity. Generally, the amount of liquid water consumed by deer is inversely proportional to the concentration of water in the food — deer drink less free water when consuming succulent green vegetation during early summer, but more during late summer when plants become more fibrous. During hot weather, deer can survive on dew, temporary water from rain puddles, or by eating moist vegetation, if available, but whitetails living in the arid Southwest may concentrate closer to permanent water areas.

DISEASES AND PARASITES

Whitetails serve as hosts to a multitude of viral, bacterial, and protozoan diseases, as well as internal and external parasites. To date, at least 111 parasite species have been identified in white-tailed deer. Certainly, summer is not the only time that deer are plagued by such maladies; hot humid weather that characterizes the summer season, especially in the South, however, is especially conducive to the transmission and spreading of diseases and parasites.

Usually, whitetails can tolerate internal and external parasites without suffering serious consequences, and disease-causing agents only rarely cause heavy mortality. There are exceptions, of course, especially when deer are malnourished or when they live at high densities. Such stressed whitetails, in particular, sometimes suffer significant mortality due to heavy parasite loads or infectious diseases. These problems are most pronounced in the South, but even northern deer occasionally suffer severe consequences.

Certainly, whitetails always have been, and likely always will be, plagued by diseases and parasites to some degree, and their wild, secretive nature excludes special measures on the part of man to totally eliminate such risk. Even so, whitetails have already incidentally benefited, in some cases, from insect eradication programs aimed to benefit domestic livestock.

As with any animal, diseases and parasites tend to be most prevalent among the poorest and weakest whitetails — especially malnourished individuals living at high density. Well-nourished, energetic whitetails, on the other hand, tend to be more resistant. Well-fed whitetails are even less likely to be plagued with heavy parasite loads, primarily because they spend more time meticulously grooming themselves to get rid of the annoying pests.

Since conventional methods employed to reduce the incidence of diseases and parasites among domestic livestock are not applicable to deer, the solution to reducing these maladies among whitetails seems rather obvious: The best alternative is to maintain deer populations in balance with range carrying capacity, thus ensuring that deer are not crowded and that they remain in good physical condition.

External parasites, especially ticks, transmit diseases in whitetail populations. Tick infestations may not be fatal in themselves, but they my lead to stress-related mortality from other causes, especially where deer live in high densities.

The hot, humid days of summer find parasites particularly plentiful and a bane to whitetail deer. In the South, summer weather is especially conducive to the transmission of parasites and diseases among whitetails.

ANTLER DEVELOPMENT

Mature hardened antlers are true bone grown only by members of the deer family, Cervidae. Antlers differ from horns in that they are branched structures, horns are not. Additionally, while growing, antlers are living tissue possessing a blood and nerve supply, whereas horns are composed of keratin, a protein secretion similar to that comprising hooves. What makes antlers so unique is that they are the only mammalian appendages that completely replace themselves on an annual basis; horns are permanent structures (except in pronghorn antelope) that grow incrementally, year by year, from the base of the animal's skull.

Antlers are seasonal structures whose growth is dependent upon rhythmic variations in the amount of daylight, which triggers the rise and fall of the male sex hormone testosterone. In whitetails, males begin growing antlers in April or May, when sex hormone production is minimal. The growth rate accelerates in June and early July, when the antler may elongate

Antlers are recognized as one the fastest growing tissues in the animal kingdom. In mid-summer, a buck's antler tips may elongate as much as a quarter of an inch per day.

The timing of antler growth is closely regulated by male hormone production, which itself is linked to seasonal changes in photoperiod, or day length.

at the rate of a quarter of an inch per day. Complete elongation of the antler is normally completed in 100 days, generally by the end of July on the northern edge of whitetail deer range.

Completion of antler growth, antler mineralization, and velvet shedding are closely linked to the shortening days of late summer. It is the sharply rising production of testosterone that induces such change and which also brings about dramatic changes in buck behavior immediately prior to the breeding season.

Research conducted by pioneer investigators George Wislocki, Joseph Aub, and Charles Waldo determined that antlers grow from the tips, not from the base, and that bone near the antlers' tips, when examined histologically, looks very much like a malignant bone tumor because of the arrangement of cells and the speed of cellular growth. The cells of the growing tip also contain a high concentration of phosphatase, the same enzyme present in growing bone and bone cancer.

"How such improbable appendages could have arisen in the first place," says Richard Goss, one of the world's leading authorities on antler regeneration, function, and evolution, "has been a challenging problem for evolutionary ecologists. The significance of antlers in the social lives of deer seems to generate theories in inverse proportion to available facts. . . . The mechanisms by which these 'bones of contention' grow and differentiate into such magnificent morphologies is a source of wonder and curiosity."

Trauma and wound healing accompany antler casting (the natural process of shedding antlers) and are especially important in the deer antler cycle. Because of this, some scientists speculate that antlers in deer evolved as a special adaptation in response to continuous forehead injury. According to fossil evidence, the early ancestors of deer had only bony protuberances, covered with hair, growing from their skulls. When used as weapons, these structures were probably vulnerable to repeated injuries. If so, natural selection may have favored animals capable of healing the wound sites in such a way so as to replace lost parts, thus giving rise to antlers.

"Whatever may have been the pathways of antler evolution," says Goss, "they were molded by the social functions for which these structures were designed. . . . Although antlers serve to advertise male rank, whether they do so by head-to-head combat or through intimidation of visual display is a matter of debate. In either case, it is clear that in the course of cervid phylogeny, antlers have evolved hand in hand with the development of specific behavior patterns in various kinds of deer."

Although the velvet skin covering a buck's antlers functionally differs from the skin covering the rest of its body, a genetic deficiency of pigment-bearing cells, as is typical of albinism, will extend to this specialized tissue.

ANTLER SIZE AND FORM

The size of a buck's rack will vary depending upon the animal's age, its nutritional history, inherited traits, and even certain psychological factors. Buck antler size and body size generally go together. That is, a healthy large-bodied buck tends to carry large antlers, whereas a small buck will more likely grow small antlers.

Antler size and body size tend to increase with a buck's age. Although buck fawns may grow small button, or infant, antlers when six to seven months old, most bucks grow their first full-fledged set of antlers when one and a half years old. A buck normally achieves his maximum body size when five or six years old and grows his largest antlers when five and a half to eight and a half years old. Antlers' deciduous nature, then, permits antlers to grow larger each year and to keep pace with increasing body size.

Although scientists debate the issue, there is often little relationship between the size of a yearling buck's antlers and the size of his antlers when he is fully grown. Yearling bucks cannot grow antlers of record book proportions, but when born on schedule and well nourished, they can grow respectable racks with eight or more points.

In some areas, yearling bucks with short spike antlers, those hardly visible above the hairline, are quite

A whitetail buck's antlers increase in mass as the animal ages and grows in body size, as seen in this buck, photographed at two and a half years and later at four and a half years of age.

common. All too often, however, these are nothing more than antlers grown by malnourished, stressed young animals, not necessarily antlers resulting from growth on bucks of inferior genetic ancestry. Spike antlers grown by older bucks are a distinct sign of poor health, most often due to inadequate nutrition.

Poor antler growth among young deer often accompanies deer overabundance, but other factors are sometimes involved. Serious depletion of nutritious plants, frequently due to foraging by too many deer, often results in poor physical development among deer, including the growth of small antlers. Sometimes, however, small antlers reflect inherent soil infertility. Steve Shea and his coworkers found range nutrition so poor for whitetails living in the flatwood habitats of northwestern Florida, for instance, that 78 percent of the yearling bucks grew spike antlers less than five inches long. Furthermore, herd reduction there did little to improve the deers' nutritional plane. Even when deer density was purposely lowered, body size and antler size among yearling bucks did not improve in Shea's study area.

Psychological stress due to overpopulation and, subsequently, the frequent conflicts that arise among deer, can also suppress antler growth among young bucks, even when nourishing foods are plentiful. Although the physiological mechanisms involved in this intriguing phenomenon are poorly understood, it appears that behavioral stress may lead to a deficiency in testosterone production or cause some type of hormonal disturbance that blocks its stimulating effects.

When two and a half to three and a half years old, most healthy bucks will grow "typical" eight- to ten-point antlers. Exceptionally well nourished older bucks, especially those raised in captivity, may grow very atypical, or "nontypical," antlers with many extra points. (Drop points grown by large bucks are sometimes genetic, inherited traits, but in other instances they tend to be spurious structures grown only occasionally and under poorly understood circumstances.)

A mature buck usually grows antlers that are remarkably similar each year. Many antler features such as rack shape, tine length, and configuration, as well as other specific features, are unquestionably hereditary. But upon reaching old age, the buck may revert to growing only forked or spike antlers. In a sense, he goes back to growing antlers more characteristic of immature bucks, which also forecasts his impending demise.

"Whether the stunted antlers of elderly deer are explained in terms of decreased sex hormone secretion or are attributable to accumulated degenerative effects of old age," says Goss, "is unknown." He emphasizes, however, that "antlers carried by senile bucks bear no resemblance to those grown by castrated deer." Instead, degenerate antlers of old bucks are more like the stunted antlers — usually thick, short spikes — sometimes produced under conditions of malnutrition.

Antler peculiarities, though, are strictly the result of chance. Heavy infestations of lung worm (*Dictoyocaus sp.*), for example, sometimes cause bucks to grow corkscrew-shaped antlers. Skeletal injury or direct injury to the tender, growing antler itself can also produce abnormal antler formation, which shouldn't be confused with malformations caused by poor nutrition, sickness, extreme old age, or genetics. A one-sided oddity in a pair of antlers is most often the result of some type of injury, whereas other abnormalities will usually show on both sides of a buck's rack. One of the most intriguing phenomena observed in antler growth is referred to as "contralateral effects," where injuries to one side of a buck's body, usually involving a leg, result in antler deformities on the opposite side. The effects may appear for several years after the injury. When the injury contributes to a permanent disability such as in the case of a leg amputation, the contralateral antler is generally shorter than normal through the remainder of the animal's life.

Reasons for contralateral effects are unknown. In fact, some scientists refute such theory altogether. Many

Serious injuries to one side of a whitetail buck's body will affect antler growth on the opposite side of its body. This intriguing phenomenon, known as "contralateral effect," may occur for several years following the injury.

Injuries to a buck's pedicle, such breaking off part of the skull when the antlers are cast (right), may result in atypical antler growth the following season.

times, uninjured deer, which appear normal and healthy, grow unequal antlers. Instances in which normal antlers are produced despite injuries are also common.

PEDICLE WOUNDS

Before any deer can grow antlers it must first grow pedicles on which the antlers form; only the pedicle is capable of giving rise to a normal and complete antler. Typically, the larger the pedicle, the larger the antler outgrowth. Injury to the pedicle may cause abnormal antler formation, or it may even lead to accessory antlers produced by the injured pedicle or nearby regions of the skull.

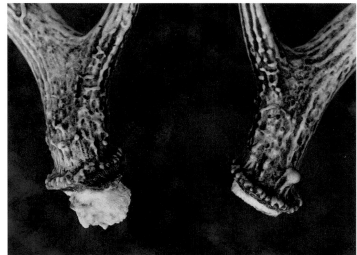

Accessory antlers are usually malformed and shorter than normal antlers. They may originate as a separate shaft from the antler base or as short spikes from the forehead region or upper orbit of the eye. Accessory antlers also tend to follow the normal antler-replacement cycle by shedding velvet in autumn, dropping off in winter, and regrowing in spring.

VELVET ANTLER INJURIES

The whitetail buck's nervous system plays a key, but mysterious, role in antler development. The growing antler is well endowed with nerves, the principle function of which must be to enable the deer to avoid injury. Also, large-antlered bucks seem to possess a certain kinesthetic sense that permits them to judge the position of their antlers and to avoid bumping them. The buck's velvet antler hairs must serve as sensitive feelers. Inevitably, however, growing antlers are sometimes damaged.

One of the most common injuries is a fracture of the antler. Sometimes the break is so severe that part of the antler dangles loosely, held only by the velvet, and eventually drops off. If the blood supply to the injured antler is not discontinued, however, the broken part may remain alive, fuse, and continue to grow at a crooked angle. If the antler is only cracked, it can repair itself.

The complete loss of a pedicle in any given year will result in no antler growth or the growth of a smaller, deformed antler on the side of the head where the injured pedicle is located.

Drop points grown by large bucks may be genetically inherited traits;
otherwise these atypical antler characteristics appear to grow only
occasionally and under poorly understood circumstances.

Injury to a velvet-covered antler sometimes results in a dislocated fracture that may remain alive, fuse, and continue to grow at a crooked angle.

Such damage generally results in conspicuous swelling along the shaft where the fracture occurred.

Experimental denerving of the growing antler usually contributes to stunted antlers with abnormal form. This results because deer cannot avoid bumping into objects in their environment and injuring their soft antlers. Sometimes, however, injury to the normal velvet-covered antler causes the growth of abnormally large, misshapen antlers. In fact, early gamekeepers in Europe reportedly sometimes shot the velvet-covered antlers of deer with shotguns to cause extra antler points to grow.

ANTLERED DOES

With the exception of reindeer and caribou, female deer normally do not grow antlers. Nonetheless, females in all species of deer are endowed with the capacity to grow antlers and sometimes do so when certain poorly understood circumstances arise. For mysterious reasons, female whitetails, mule deer, and roe deer tend to grow antlers much more frequently than do the females of most other cervid species. In fact, antlered female whitetails are more common than most people realize.

In New York State, for example, William Severinghaus estimated a frequency of one antlered doe per 2,650 whitetail bucks harvested during the period from 1941 to 1955. Researchers in Pennsylvania reported one antlered doe per 3,500 bucks harvested in the state from 1958 until 1961. In Michigan, biologists examining hunter-harvested deer found nine antlered does among 8,605 adult does (one antlered doe per 956 bucks) examined from 1959 to 1961. For a national average, it has been estimated that one in every 1,000 to 1,100 female whitetails might produce antlers.

Without question, the most amazing documentation of antlered female whitetails was made by William Wishart in Camp Wainwright, a 965 square mile military reserve located in eastern Alberta, Canada. While monitoring hunter harvest of whitetails on the area, Wishart recorded an incidence of antlered does 15 to 40 times higher than those reported by previous investigators.

During a 15-year period (1968-1982), Wishart examined 1,182 adult whitetails harvested by hunters on the Wainwright area, including 665 bucks and 517 does. Eight of the adult does had antlers ranging from about six-tenths of an inch to nearly nine and a half inches long. All of the doe antlers were still velvet covered, at a time when all bucks carried polished antlers. This amounts to an astonishing rate of one antlered doe among every 65 adult does, or one antlered doe per every 83 adult bucks.

Based largely upon 19th century European research conducted on roe deer, George Wislocki proposed that antlered does fall into various groups, depending upon the status of their reproductive tracts, as follows:

1) No recognizable pathology and a seemingly normal female reproductive tract.
2) Diseased or degenerate ovaries, usually from unknown causes.
3) Degenerate ovaries caused by old age.
4) True hermaphrodites having both ovaries and testes but possessing either male or female external sex organs or both.
5) Pseudohermaphrodites (also called cryptorchid males) with abdominal (internal) rudimentary testes and no recognizable ovaries.

Descriptions of doe antlers include velvet-covered pedicles only, or small "button" antlers; small velvet-covered spikes with occasional branching; and hard, polished antlers as usually occur in bucks. European investigators observed that the relative size and characteristics of doe antlers varied depending upon the type of reproductive tract the deer possessed. Does with ovaries, for example, showed the least amount of antler development. True hermaphrodites generally had a greater amount of antler development, whereas pseudohermaphrodites showed the greatest amount of antler development.

Some antlered does are capable of breeding and rearing fawns, some are not. Of does bearing antlers, fertile does carry velvet-covered antlers. It is important to note that comparatively high levels of testosterone are required to promote antler hardening and velvet stripping. As in the case of male castrates, otherwise sexually normal female whitetails seldom achieve such elevated levels of male sex hormone production; hence, they tend to carry velvet-covered antlers throughout the fall season. Although there seems to be little reliable data for wild deer, the so-called antlered doe with polished antlers probably exhibits rather sharp seasonal changes in male hormone production and probably casts its antlers annually.

Researchers have successfully induced antler growth in female deer in various ways. Wislocki first made whitetail does grow antlers by removing their ovaries, then injecting single "priming" doses of testosterone. Later, Bubenik stimulated pedicle growth in female whitetails by administering drugs that blocked the production of the female hormone estrogen. He then followed up with surgical injury to the forehead bones to produce antler growth.

What causes the growth of antlers in otherwise normal female whitetails is unknown. Some researchers suggest the ability to produce antlers may be inherited.

In any given population of whitetails, a number of does will develop velvet-covered pedicles, and others will grow velvet-covered antlers. Most of these females are fertile and capable of bearing young.

Others believe a brief imbalance in sex hormones is involved. Still others propose accidental injury to the forehead area of a female can cause antler growth.

Wishart was unable to explain the unusually high incidence of antlered does at Camp Wainwright. However, all of those he examined belonged to the fertile velvet-spike group and were quite old (averaging over six years). Older does more likely have degenerate ovaries, adrenal tumors, or other maladies that cause hormonal imbalances possibly responsible for producing male characteristics. Adrenal tumors, in particular, are known to cause increased production of male sex hormones and masculinizing traits in females of other species.

The growth of pedicles, and subsequently antlers, in deer is dependent upon short-term elevations in the secretion of the male hormone testosterone. Since the ovaries of female mammals are known to produce a limited amount of male hormone, Wislocki speculated that ovarian production of male hormones may sometimes trigger antler growth. He suggested that antlered female deer with functional ovaries may have secreted either male hormones or progesterone during pregnancy and that these hormones triggered the pituitary gland, prompting antler growth. Such a short burst of male sex hormone could stimulate antler growth and produce permanently fixed velvet-covered antlers, but still not interfere with subsequent breeding and fawn rearing.

It has been observed that administering testosterone to female deer sometimes produces pedicles, but not antler growth. It is then necessary to surgically "injure" the pedicles to cause antler growth. Interestingly, if one pedicle is injured, but not the other, only the injured side will produce an antler. This implies, therefore, that the nervous system is also somehow intricately involved.

Some "true" female deer grow only one antler, but others grow a paired set. Hence, it is tempting to implicate forehead injury in the growth of single antlers, but to an imbalance in sex hormone production when females grow two antlers.

"The presence of antlers in female deer," says Goss, "is a reminder of how fragile the distinction between the sexes can be. Although the gender of an individual is genetically determined, the extent to which sexual characteristics are in fact expressed may be affected by a number of physiological conditions."

The "freemartin" is a prime example of how the sex of an animal can be modified even before birth. A freemartin is a female calf born co-twin to a male. In about eleven out of twelve cases the female is sterile, because her reproductive system has been modified by her brother's sex hormones.

Goss explains the complex phenomenon, which takes place in the womb, this way: "Sometimes the placenta of such twins becomes fused, as a result of which their bloodstreams intermingle. When the male twin begins to develop its reproductive tract, the hormones produced can circulate into his sister's bloodstream and exert effects on the development of her reproductive organs. As a result of this, she may become a partially masculinized female and therefore infertile."

Although the freemartin typically occurs in cattle, Goss proposes that antlered does might have been subjected to similar male hormonal influences before they were born. He admits there is no proof of freemartins in deer, but is quick to note that antlered does occur most frequently in those deer species that commonly produce twins, whereas they are rare among others that normally produce only a single fawn.

"An intriguing phenomenon indeed," says Goss, "one that demands explanation." But with the possibility of intersexual characteristics involved, the subject becomes highly complex and cannot be resolved without careful examination of the so-called antlered doe's reproductive tract. Generally, however, if the animal in question has polished antlers, it quite likely is not a true female.

ANTLER MATURATION

The antler is an outgrowth of bone from the pedicle, the place on the base of the skull from which the antler grows, whereas skin overlying the pedicle gives rise to antler velvet that covers and feeds the growing antler. Initially, the developing antler is fed by blood vessels arising internally, originating within the pedicle, as well as via the velvet.

Antler velvet differs from the skin and hair that cover the deer's body. George Bubenik describes velvet as a "modified skin with modified pelage," or a special type of "fur." Velvet grows anew each year, after the antlers drop off, from the ring of skin that surrounds the wound left by the cast antler. Antler velvet is richly supplied with blood vessels and nerves and is capable of enormous expansion, necessary to keep pace with the antler's rapid growth rate. The velvet skin has no muscles, but associated with each hair follicle on the velvet is a sebaceous gland from which an oily secretion, sebum, is produced. Sebum is responsible for the shiny appearance of the velvet skin, a condition which becomes more obvious when the velvet starts to shrink and die, forcing droplets of sebum to the surface.

Hardening of the antler appears to happen suddenly, but it is actually a gradual process. The outer surface of the antler hardens rather quickly in the few weeks before

velvet shedding. However, mineral deposition in the interior of the antler is a more gradual and prolonged process. Bone formation starts internally in lower portions of the antler during early stages of antler development, progressing from the base to tips as the antlers elongate.

Blood flow from the pedicle into the antler core becomes restricted by midsummer as the pedicles become semimineralized. Hence, during its second half of growth, the antler is nourished primarily by the velvet's superficial temporal artery and a dozen or so of its major branches. It is the shutting off of blood flow through these vessels that leads to velvet death, drying, and, eventually, shedding of the velvet and death of the antler. Even after velvet shedding, impressions of these arteries are visible in the antler bone as molded channels.

The final demise of antler velvet starts with a thickening and hardening of the velvet's arterial walls,

Velvet grows at the same rapid rate as the antlers they cover. The four-year-old buck pictured here, photographed in April, May, June, and July of the same year, demonstrates the implausible rate at which both antlers and their protective covering can develop.

due to deposition of mineral salts that interfere with blood flow — a condition similar to arteriosclerosis. As a result, blood flow decreases sharply as openings in the arteries constrict. According to theory, the sympathetic nervous system then responds by completely shutting off blood flow to the velvet, causing the starved velvet to die. Velvet death normally takes several weeks, but sometimes strangulation of blood flow to the velvet can occur suddenly.

Given the circumstances surrounding velvet death, Goss concludes: "The seasonal demise of antler skin is not innately programmed to death of its cells, but must be attributed to external agencies . . . the shedding of antler velvet, therefore, is a case of murder, not suicide."

Death and stripping of the antler velvet generally signals death of the antler core itself. However, since the velvet may die before the antler tips harden, George Bubenik theorizes that death of the velvet and death of the antler may be separate processes.

Even after shedding of the velvet, the innermost portions of the antler may remain porous, retaining a trickle of blood flow into the base of the antler. Eventually, however, even the spongy core of the antler will dry out as it becomes converted to solid bone. Then the antler literally dies back to the junction of the pedicle. Such change over time probably explains why

Usually, bucks strip their velvet within 24 hours. When the process is nearly complete but loose strips of velvet remain attached to a buck's antlers, he may try to chew or scratch them away from the antler base.

antlers become more brittle toward the end of the rut, immediately before they are cast.

As antlers harden, they shrink; so does the drying velvet, which tends to split lengthwise. In some cases, the dry condition may persist for days before the buck finally starts rubbing off the dead velvet. What exactly prompts the buck to then suddenly rub his antlers on vegetation or any other object, peeling off the dead antler covering, is unknown.

Since the live velvet is well supplied with nerves, some people believe dead or dying velvet causes irritation or itching, thereby resulting in the bucks' rubbing response. Even many scientists hold this view. Sometimes, however, rubbing may occur prematurely, when the velvet is still living, or even before the antler is fully hardened, which causes heavy bleeding. Rubbing of living velvet has also been observed after experimental denervation of the antlers negates the possibility of any sensations whatsoever.

George Bubenik contends that the rubbing of velvet occurs relatively independent of antler mineralization. He suggests rubbing is primarily a behavioral response triggered by sharply rising levels of male sex hormones, which stimulate the central nervous system. Certainly, such is the case once bucks carry hardened antlers and use them to make rubs that serve as signposts. Some highly aggressive bucks even continue rubbing with their foreheads after casting their antlers.

Most often, velvet stripping is accomplished within 24 hours. But sometimes the process of cleaning antlers of velvet may be accomplished within less than an hour, or at other times it may encompass several days.

Occasionally the rub-out is incomplete, with live velvet left clinging to lower portions of the antlers for days or even weeks. Such incomplete rubbing is especially common among injured, diseased, or senile bucks, presumably due to low production of male hormones.

Strips of velvet left hanging from the antler base seem to irritate a buck, causing him to shake his head vigorously. In some cases the buck might even eat the limp dangling strips or use his feet to carefully scratch away remnants of velvet that cling stubbornly to the antler base.

Newly exposed antlers are nearly pure white but become darker in color after frequent rubbing against trees and shrubs. Some investigators claim dried blood left on the antler following initial rub-out stains the antlers. However, since pen-raised bucks deprived of frequent rubbing opportunities often carry abnormally light-colored antlers, I'm inclined to believe antlers of wild bucks are darkened primarily from the bark juices of the trees and shrubs they rub.

The precise timing of velvet death varies among bucks, depending upon their age, physical condition, dominance rank, and no doubt numerous other factors that interact to determine seasonal rhythms in sex hormone levels. Any stressful condition such as poor diet, injury, disease, heavy parasite load, extreme old age, or social stress would likely suppress or delay an individual buck's seasonal rise in testosterone output and delay velvet stripping. Late-born yearling bucks, in particular, tend to rub off velvet later than older healthy bucks. Velvet shedding schedules also vary regionally.

On northern range, bucks commence rubbing during the last week of August, with peak rubbing activity occurring during early September. Undersized yearlings with abnormally small (short spike) antlers or unhealthy older individuals may not complete rubbing until mid-October. Only rarely do bucks in the Upper Great Lakes region or in the Northeast carry velvet antlers into November.

On the other hand, researchers in Mississippi report that captive bucks shed velvet from September 4 to October 12, the average being September 24. These biologists also observed wide variation in shedding date by individual bucks from one year to the next and saw some wild bucks carrying velvet-covered antlers in mid-

December. Velvet shedding schedules are even more variable in southern Texas.

Studies conducted at the University of Georgia demonstrated that yearling and two-and-one-half-year-old bucks exhibit delayed elevations in testosterone production and entered rutting condition later than older males. Normally, bucks four and a half to eight and a half years old exhibit the earliest rise in testosterone and attain the highest levels of hormone production. This probably explains why young bucks, even in the absence of older bucks, tend to make fewer rubs and scrapes and show delayed rubbing when compared with older individuals.

The Georgia studies also revealed that dominance-submissive relationships become very important in determining the order of velvet shedding among bucks in any given population. Dominant bucks shed velvet earlier than subordinates, regardless of age. In the wild, older bucks normally dominate younger ones and shed velvet first. But even in the absence of older bucks, superior young bucks will be the first to carry velvet-free antlers.

These findings illustrate the importance of behavior and support the view that male whitetail "winners" become physiologically and psychologically stimulated. Bucks that win dominance are often the first to become hormonally charged, shed antler velvet first, and become avid scent markers. Logically, habitual "losers" suffer the opposite, depressing effects.

Regionally, whatever the precise timing may be, velvet shedding is a prelude to coming events — sharp seasonal changes in white-tailed deer behavior are about to take place. Velvet shedding signals the death of antlers, an end to the tranquil days of whitetail summer, and the arrival of that special, hectic time of year — whitetail autumn.

Antlers of younger males begin growing later and at a slower rate than those of older bucks. Compare the one-year-old buck pictured here in mid-May, and on page 141 in early September and in November, with the four-year-old buck on pages 136-137.

SELECTED REFERENCES

Atkeson, T. D., R. L. Marchinton, and K. V. Miller. 1988. Vocalizations of white-tailed deer. *American Midland Nat.* 120:194-200.

Beier, P. 1987. Sex differences in quality of white-tailed deer diets. *J. Mammal.* 68:323-329.

Brown, B. A., Jr. 1974. Social organization in male groups of white-tailed deer. in V. Geist and F. Walther eds., *The behavior of ungulates and its relation to management*, pp. 436-446. 2 vol. New Series Publ. 23 Morges, Switzerland:IUCN. 940 pp.

Brown, R. D., ed. 1988. *Antler development in Cervidae.* Caesar Kleberg Wildl. Res. Inst., Kingsville, TX. 480 pp.

Bubenik, G. A., and A. B. Bubenik, eds. 1990. *Horns, pronghorns, and antlers: evolution, morphology, physiology, and social significance.* Springer-Verlag, New York Inc., 562 pp.

Chapman, D. I. 1975. Antlers — bones of contention. *Mammal Rev.* 5:121-172.

Darling, F. F. 1937. *A herd of red deer: A study in animal behavior.* London: Oxford University Press. 215 pp.

Davidson, W. R., F. A. Hayes, V. F. Nettles, and F. E. Kellogg, eds. 1981. *Diseases and parasites of white-tailed deer.* Tallahassee, FL: Tall Timbers Research Station. 458 pp.

Donaldson, J. C., and J. K. Doutt. 1965. Antlers in female white-tailed deer: a 4-year study. *J. Wildl. Mgmt.* 29:699-705.

Forand, K. J., and R. L. Marchinton. 1989. Patterns of social grooming in adult white-tailed deer. *Amer. Midland Nat.* 122:357-364.

Forand, K. J., R. L. Marchinton, and K. V. Miller. 1985. Influence of dominance rank on the antler cycle of white-tailed. *J. Mammal.* 66:58-62.

Gerlach, D., S. Atwater, and J. Schnell (Eds.). 1994. *Deer.* Stackpole Books, Mechanicsburg, PA. 384 pp.

Goss, R. J. 1983. *Deer antlers: regeneration, function, and evolution.* Academic Press, NY. 316 pp.

Halls, L. K., ed. 1984. *White-tailed deer: ecology and management.* Wildl. Manage. Inst., Stackpole Co., Harrisburg, PA. 870 pp.

Haugen, A. O., and D. W. Speake. 1958. Determining age of young fawn white-tailed deer. *J. Wildl. Mgmt.* 22:319-321.

Hesselton, W. T., and R. M. Hesselton. 1982. White-tailed deer. Pages 878-901 in J. A. Chapman and G. A. Feldhamer, eds. *Wild mammals of North America.* The John Hopkins University Press, Baltimore, ME

Hirth, D. H. 1977. Observations of loss of antler velvet in white-tailed deer. *Southwestern Nat.* 22:269-286.

Hirth, D. H. 1985. Mother-young behavior in white-tailed deer, *Odocoileus virginianus. Southwestern Naturalist* 30:297-302.

Hirth, D. H., and D. R. McCullough. 1977. Evolution of alarm signals in ungulates with special reference to white-tailed deer. *American Nat.* 111:31-42.

Holzenbein, S., and R. L. Marchinton. 1992. Spatial integration of maturing-male white-tailed deer into the adult population. *J. Mammal.* 73:326-334.

Inglis, J. M., R. E. Hood, B. A. Brown, and C. A. DeYoung. 1979. Home range of white-tailed deer in Texas coastal prairie brushland. *J. Mammal.* 60:377-389.

Jacobsen, N. K. 1984. Changes in 24-hour activity patterns with growth of white-tailed deer fawns *(Odocoileus viginianus). J. Interdiscipl. Cycle Res.* 15:213-226.

Jackson, R. 1972. Activity patterns of young white-tailed deer fawns in South Texas. *J. Ecol.* 53:262-270.

Lent, P. C. 1974. Mother-infant relationships in ungulates. in V. Geist and F. Walther eds., *The behavior of ungulates and its relation to management.* pp. 14-55. 1 vol. New Series Publ. 24. Morges, Switzerland: IUCN, 940 pp.

McCullough, D. R. 1979. *The George Reserve deer herd: population ecology of a K-selected species.* Ann Arbor: Michigan Univ. Press. 271 pp.

McCullough, D. R. 1985. Variables influencing food habits of white-tailed deer on the George Reserve. *J. Mammal.* 66: 682-692.

Michael, E. D. 1968. Playing by white-tailed deer in South Texas. *Amer. Midland Nat.* 80:535-537

Miller, K. V., and R. L. Marchinton eds. 1995. *Quality whitetails: the why and how of quality deer management.* Stackpole Books, PA. 322 pp.

Miller, K. V., R. L. Marchinton, J. R. Beckwith, aand P. B. Bush. 1985. Variations in density and chemical composition of white-tailed deer antlers. *J. Mammal.* 66:693-701.

Moen, A. N., M. A. DellaFerra, A. L. Hiller, and B. A. Buxton. 1978. Heart rates of white-tailed deer fawns in response to recorded wolf howls. *Canadian J. Zool.* 56:1207-1210.

Nelson, M. E., and L. D. Mech. 1990. Weights, productivity, and mortality of old white-tailed deer. *J. Mammal.* 71: 689-691.

Nelson, M. E., and L. D. Mech. 1981. Deer social organization and wolf predation in northeastern Minnesota. *Wildl. Monogr.* 77, 53pp.

Nelson, M. E., and L. D. Mech. 1984. Home range formation and dispersal of deer in northeastern Minnesota. *J. Mammal.* 65: 567-575.

Nelson, M. E., and L. D. Mech. 1990.

Nelson, T. A., and A. Woolf. 1985. Birth size and growth of deer fawns in southern Illinois. *J. Wildl. Mgmt.* 49:374-377.

Nixon, C. M., L. P. Hansen, P. A. Brewer, and J. E. Chelsvig. 1991. Ecology of white-tailed deer in an intensively farmed region of Illinois. *Wildl. Monogr.* 118, 77 pp.

Nixon, C. M., L. P. Hansen, P. A. Brewer, and J. E. Chelsvig. 1992. Stability of white-tailed doe parturition ranges on a refuge in east-central Illinois. *Canadian J. Zool.* 70:968 973.

Ozoga, J. J. 1988. Incidence of "infant" antlers among supplementally-fed white-tailed deer. *J. Mammal.* 69:393-395.

Ozoga, J. J., and L. J. Verme. 1982. Physical and reproductive characteristics of a supplementally-fed white-tailed deer herd. *J. Wildl. Mgmt.* 46:281-301.

Ozoga, J. J., and L. J. Verme. 1984. Effects of family bond deprivation on reproductive performance in female white-tailed deer. *J. Wildl. Mgmt.* 48:1326-1334.

Ozoga, J. J., and L. J. Verme. 1985. Comparative breeding behavior and performance of yearlings vs. prime-age white-tailed bucks. *J. Wildl. Mgmt.* 49:364-372.

Ozoga, J. J., and L. J. Verme. 1986. Initial and subsequent maternal success of white-tailed deer. *J. Wildl. Mgmt.* 50: 122-124.

Ozoga, J. J., and L. J. Verme. 1986. Relation of maternal age to fawn-rearing success in white-tailed deer. *J. Wildl. Mgmt.* 50:480-486.

Ozoga, J. J., L. J. Verme, and C. S. Bienz. 1982. Parturition behavior and territoriality in white-tailed deer: impact on neonatal mortality. *J. Wildl. Mgmt.* 46:1-11.

Rawson, R. E., G. D. DelGiudice, H. E. Dziuk, and L. D. Mech. 1992. Energy metabolism and hematology of white-tailed deer fawns. *J. Wildl. Disease.* 28:91-94.

Richardson, L. W., H. A. Jacobson, R. J. Muncy, and C. J. Perkins 1983. Acoustics of white-tailed deer *(Odocoileus virginianus). J. Mammal.* 64:245-252.

Robbins, C. T., and A. N. Moen. 1975. Milk consumption and weight gain of white-tailed deer. *J. Wildl. Mgmt.* 39:355-360.

Rogers, L. L., J. J. Mooty, and D. Dawson. 1981. *Foods of white-tailed deer in the Upper Great Lakes Region — a review.* USDA Forest Service, General Technical Report NC-65. USDA Forest Service, St. Paul MN. 24 pp.

Rue, L. L. III. 1989. *The deer of North America.* 2nd edition, updated and expanded. Outdoor Life Books. Grolier Book Clubs Inc., Danbury, CT. 508 pp.

Ryel, L. A. 1963. The occurrence of certain anomalies in Michigan white-tailed deer. *J. Mammal.* 44:79-98.

Schultz, S. R., and M. K. Johnson. 1992. Chronology of antler velvet shedding in captive Louisiana white-tailed deer. *J. Wildl. Mgmt.* 56:651-655.

Severinghaus, C. W. 1956. Antlered does. *New York State Conservationist* 10:32.

Shea, S. M., T. A. Brault, and M. L. Richardson. 1992. Herd density and physical condition of white-tailed deer in Florida flatwoods. *J. Wildl. Mgmt.* 56:262-267.

Shope, R. E., L. G. MacNamara, and R. Mangold. 1955. Report on the deer mortality: epizootic hemorrhagic disease of deer. *New Jersey Outdoors* 6: 15-21.

Short, H. L. 1964. Postnatal stomach development of white-tailed deer. *J. Wildl. Mgmt.* 28:445-458.

Schwede, G., H. Hendrichs, and C. Wemmer. 1994. Early mother-young relations in white-tailed deer. *J. Mammal.* 75:438-445.

Schwede, G., H. Hendrichs, and W. McShea. 1993. Social and spatial organization of female white-tailed deer, *Odocoileus virginianus,* during the fawning period. *Animal Behav.* 45:1007 1017.

Seton, E. T. 1899. *The trail of the Sandhill stag.* New York: Scribners. 93 pp.

Stormer, F. A., and W. A. Bauer. 1980. Summer forage use by tame deer in northern Michigan. *J. Wildl. Mgmt.* 44:98-106.

VanDeelen, T. R. 1995. *Seasonal migrations and mortality of white-tailed deer in Michigan's Upper Peninsula.* PhD. Thesis Michigan State Univ., East Lansing. 158 pp.

Verme, L. J. 1963. Effects of nutrition on growth of white-tailed deer fawns. *Trans. North Am. Wildl. Conf.* 28:431-443.

Verme, L. J. 1985. Birth weights of fawns from doe fawn white-tailed deer. *J. Wildl. Mgmt.* 49:962-963.

Verme, L. J., and J. J. Ozoga. 1987. Relationship of photoperiod to puberty in doe fawn white-tailed deer. *J. Mammal.* 68:107 -110.

Whitehead, G. K. 1993. *The Whitehead encyclopedia of deer.* Voyageur Press. Stillwater, MN. 597 pp.

Wislocki, G. B. 1954. Antlers in female deer, with a report of three cases in Odocoileus. *J. Mammal.* 35:486-495.